An Economic Appraisal of Pension Tax Policy in the United States

Other publications of the
PENSION RESEARCH COUNCIL

Concepts of Actuarial Soundness in Pension Plans—*Dorrance C. Bronson*

Social Aspects of Retirement—*Otto Pollak*

Positive Experiences in Retirement—*Otto Pollak*

Ensuring Medical Care for the Aged—*Mortimer Spiegelman*

Legal Protection of Private Pension Expectations—*Edwin W. Patterson*

Legal Status of Employee Benefit Rights under Private Pension Plans—*Benjamin Aaron*

Decision and Influence Processes in Private Pension Plans—*James E. McNulty, Jr.*

Fulfilling Pension Expectations—*Dan M. McGill*

Collectively Bargained Multiemployer Pension Plans—*Joseph J. Melone*

Actuarial Aspects of Pension Security—*William F. Marples*

Status of Funding under Private Pension Plans—*Frank L. Griffin, Jr.*, and *Charles L. Trowbridge* (out of print)

Guaranty Fund for Private Pension Obligations—*Dan M. McGill*

Preservation of Pension Benefit Rights—*Dan M. McGill*

Retirement Systems for Public Employees—*Thomas P. Bleakney*

Employer Guarantee of Pension Benefits—*Dan M. McGill*

Reciprocity among Private Multiemployer Pension Plans—*Maurice E. McDonald*

A New Look at Accounting for Pension Costs—*William D. Hall* and *David L. Landsittel*

Social Security and Private Pension Plans: Competitive or Complementary? *Dan M. McGill* (ed.)

Pension Mathematics—*Howard E. Winklevoss*

Indexation of Pension and Other Benefits—*Robert J. Myers*

Joint Trust Pension Plans—*Daniel F. McGinn*

Financing the Civil Service Retirement System—*Dan M. McGill* (ed.)

Continuing Care Retirement Communities—*Howard E. Winklevoss* and *Alwyn V. Powell*

Social Investing—*Dan M. McGill* (ed.)

Employer Accounting for Pensions—*E. L. Hicks* and *C. L. Trowbridge*

Pensions, Economics and Public Policy—*Richard A. Ippolito*

Search for a National Retirement Income Policy—*Jack L. VanDerhei* (ed.)

Inflation and Pensions—*Susan M. Wachter*

Pension Asset Management: An International Perspective—*Leslie Hannah* (ed.)

Fundamentals of Private Pensions, 6th ed.—*Dan M. McGill* and *Donald S. Grubbs, Jr.*

The Economics of Pension Insurance—*Richard A. Ippolito*

It's My Retirement Money—Take Good Care of It—*William C. Greenough*

An Economic Appraisal of Pension Tax Policy in the United States

Richard A. Ippolito
Chief Economist
Pension Benefit Guaranty Corporation

Published for the
Pension Research Council
Wharton School
University of Pennsylvania
by

IRWIN

Homewood, IL 60430
Boston, MA 02116

Sponsoring editor: Michael W. Junior
Project editor: Margaret A. Schmidt
Production manager: Ann Cassady
Compositor: Compset, Inc.
Typeface: 10/12 Melior
Printer: Arcata Graphics/Kingsport

Library of Congress Cataloging-in-Publication Data

Ippolito, Richard A.
An economic appraisal of pension tax policy in the United States / Richard A. Ippolito.
p. cm.
"Published for the Pension Research Council, Wharton School, University of Pennsylvania."
Includes bibliographical references.
ISBN 0-256-08544-7
1. Pensions—Taxation—United States. 2. Old age pensions—Taxation—United States. I. Wharton School. Pension Research Council. II. Title.
HJ4653.P5I66 1990
336.24′2—dc20 89–26875
CIP

Printed in the United States of America
1 2 3 4 5 6 7 8 9 0 K 7 6 5 4 3 2 1 0

To my parents, Frank and Cecile Ippolito,
with love and gratitude.

MEMBERS OF THE PENSION RESEARCH COUNCIL

STRUCTURE AND ROLE OF THE COUNCIL

Founded in 1952, the Pension Research Council is one of several research organizations within the Wharton School of the University of Pennsylvania. As part of the nation's first school of business, the Council functions in a bracing environment of academic freedom and objectivity. The basic purpose of the Council is to undertake research that will have the effect of strengthening those arrangements designed to provide the financial resources needed for a secure and dignified old age. It seeks to broaden public understanding of these complex arrangements through basic research into their social, economic, legal, actuarial, and financial foundations. Although geared to the long view of the pension institution, projects undertaken by the Council are always relevant to real-world concerns and frequently focus on issues under current debate.

The Council is composed of individuals from large corporate plan sponsors, organized labor, actuarial consulting firms, the accounting profession, the legal profession, investment counselors, banks, insurance companies, not-for-profit organizations, and several academic disciplines. The Council does not speak with one voice and espouses no particular point of view. The members do share a general desire to encourage and strengthen private sector approaches to old age and economic security, while recognizing the essential role of Social Security and other income maintenance programs in the public sector.

The members of the Council are appointed by the Dean of the Wharton School and serve indeterminate terms. The Council reviews the findings of current research projects, acts to generate new research proposals, and reviews external proposals. In performing these functions, the members identify areas in which additional research is needed, consider the general form the research should take, then evaluate the qualifications of persons deemed capable of carrying out the approved projects.

The research projects are carried out by persons commissioned under individually designed ad hoc arrangements. The researchers are normally academic scholars, but non-academic experts with special qualifications for the tasks involved may be used. The research findings are reviewed by members of the Council, who may offer criticism as to both the substance of the report and the inferences drawn from the studies. The author of any manuscript is free to accept or reject the criticisms of the Council members, but the latter have the privilege of recording in the published document their dissent from any interpretative statements or points of view expressed by the author. Whether or not written dissents are included, publication should not be interpreted to indicate either agreement or disagreement by the Council or its individual members with the substance of the document or its inferences.

Preface

This monograph addresses the appropriate tax treatment of pensions in the United States. Except for analysis of recent changes in technical pension tax provisions, the arguments draw on the existing economics literature. The novelty of this book lies in its treatment of pensions in the tax code as part of an overall national retirement policy, including pension tax rules, pension regulations, the social security system, and individual retirement accounts. The volume evaluates these institutions against a hypothetical national retirement policy that puts the government in the role of maximizing the freedom of individuals and firms to generate the distribution of retirement ages and retirement consumption that best suits their needs.

Changes over the past 10 years in the social security system, as well as the essence of pension tax policy, conform to this hypothetical policy, likely resulting in large welfare gains for U.S. workers. A substantial portion of this volume is devoted to identifying other changes in tax policy and regulation that would more completely transform existing institutions to be consistent with the above notion of a national retirement policy. If these changes are made, labor productivity and workers' well-being could increase significantly. Yet these changes would not require the government to abandon its current policies requiring all workers to participate in some retirement income system, and transferring some monies from higher- to lower-income workers. In addition, the changes would not reduce federal tax revenue. Less pension regulation and more individual freedom can be consistent with these policy goals because important changes have occurred in the social security and tax-collection systems that make many of the original tax-related pension regulations outmoded today.

The views expressed in this volume are highly personalized. Other policy analysts, even those who might subscribe to my hypothetical national retirement policy, likely would disagree with some of the specifics of my prescriptions. Others who believe in a more interventionist government undoubtedly will have stronger disagreements with the overall thrust of my conclusions. Nevertheless, it was my hope that, by bringing together the various parts of the overall retirement system, analyzing them against a single theme, and bringing to light some of the more esoteric aspects of pension tax law, a framework would be created to help others think about optimal pension and retirement policy from perhaps a different perspective. Needless to say, the views I express do not represent the official views of the Pension Benefit Guaranty Corporation.

Richard A. Ippolito

ACKNOWLEDGMENTS

I owe a debt of gratitude to numerous individuals who directly or indirectly helped me develop this volume. First, and foremost, I would like to thank Carolyn Weaver for suggesting the idea to me, and for providing much-needed guidance on an early version. I would also like to express my appreciation to Dan McGill and Jack VanDerhei for providing intellectual and technical support for my continuing research on pensions, and for reviewing in detail earlier versions of this monograph. Also, I would like to thank other members of the Pension Research Council who provided comments indirectly to me, and who supported publication of the volume despite their own misgivings about some of my policy conclusions.

Finally, I would like to thank my many colleagues at the U.S. Department of Labor, the Pension Benefit Guaranty Corporation, and other agencies in the federal government for contributing hundreds of hours of their time trying to teach me about the details of pension tax policy and related regulatory and retirement policy issues. These individuals are too numerous to list, but I would be remiss if I did not make special mention of David Lindeman, who during his tenure at the Congressional Budget Office and as a colleague at the PBGC, spent many sessions teaching me and debating with me esoteric pension tax topics and their implications for public policy. His previous volume (with Larry Ozanne) on pension tax policy was an indispensable source for my work on pension taxation.

Contents

LIST OF TABLES

LIST OF FIGURES

CHAPTER 1

Introductory Issues

OVERVIEW

This monograph is concerned with tax policy and private pensions. The relationship between these two subjects is old and deep. Basic tax rules pertaining to pensions were established in the Internal Revenue Act of 1926. The Act provides that if firms set aside monies to provide employees' pensions, their contributions are tax deductible at the corporate level and may accumulate in tax-exempt trust funds. Contributions are taxed to workers when taken as pension benefits during retirement.

In effect, pension savings are subject to a consumption tax of sorts. This treatment is not "special" compared to the tax treatment of earnings used to support immediate consumption: these earnings also are taxed once. But it is special compared to ordinary savings, which are subject to a double tax: they are assessed an income tax at the time wages are earned and again as workers essentially try to maintain the purchasing power[1] of their savings over time.

Without special treatment in the tax code, it is doubtful that pensions would be an important institution in the United States today. It is almost certain that, without pensions, workers now and in the future would not retire at current retirement ages and could not maintain existing standards of living during retirement.

This treatise is not intended to challenge the notion that pensions matter; they matter a lot. But rather, this book examines whether or not existing tax policy is the "right" social policy and, if so, why. In attempting to answer the question, I presume that the proper role of government is not to determine for workers when they will retire and how much consumption they will enjoy during retirement, but precisely the opposite. Subject to the overall need to raise tax revenue and to prevent "spenders" from free riding on "savers," the government's role is to create an environment in which individuals are free to choose when they will stop work from their main jobs and how much they will save for retirement. I will show that this approach works in the direction of maximizing the overall benefits of workers over their lifetimes. These benefits include higher productivity and, thus, higher wages; a redistribution of consumption from work years to retirement; a better allocation of leisure time over workers' lifetimes; and in particular, longer retirement in place of shorter work weeks.

A timely question is whether current pension tax policy is appropriate. During the 1980s, mostly in response to large federal budget deficits, Congress began to evaluate whether the nation can "afford" the institution of tax-exempt pension trust funds. For example, the U.S. Joint Committee on Taxation estimates that special tax policy towards pensions reduced potential federal tax revenues by $49 billion in 1988, a time when the federal budget deficit was approximately $150 billion.[2] Indeed, Congress has taken unprecedented steps in recent years to reduce the revenue losses from pension tax policy.[3] Now is an opportune time to evaluate the economic implications of any changes in public policy towards pensions before proceeding further down this path.

In this chapter, I begin by providing some basic building blocks that are important to understanding and evaluating pension tax policy. These include how pension plans work (and how to differentiate between the basic types of pension plans); how these plans are financed (and how they might affect labor productivity); and how a tax policy that gives tax-exempt status to pension savings accounts is important in qualitative terms. Within this framework, the ensuing chapters begin the task of evaluating federal tax policy towards pensions.

It is somewhat of a misnomer to label federal tax rules towards pensions as "tax expenditure." In reality, federal rules merely represent a means of enforcing statutory marginal income tax rates in the Internal Revenue Code. Without "special" tax treatment of pension trust funds, marginal income tax rates would increase by an order of magnitude for earnings set aside for retirement consumption. This increase would greatly add to the "price" of consumption during retirement compared to work years, with the predictable consequences being later retirement and lower consumption during retirement.

It will be shown below that existing pension tax policy works to get the government out of the business of influencing retirement decisions. Doing so is consistent with recent legislation altering the nature of the social security system. Overall, current trends suggest an emerging national retirement policy that leaves most retirement decisions to the private market. Much of this book evaluates other government rules towards pensions in light of this policy, recognizing the implicit constraint that Congress will not permit pension trust funds to be used for nonpension purposes.

Much of the pension regulatory apparatus was erected to prevent "overuse" of pension trust funds and to encourage transfers from high-income workers to (or forced savings by) low-wage individuals. But this regulation has largely become outmoded owing to new tax-monitoring technology, new laws to directly control maximum tax-preferred pension income, and a nearly universal social security system that provides dramatically higher wage replacement rates to nearly all workers earning low wages over their lifetimes. Eliminating the now redundant regulations on pension plans can lift a large burden from workers and firms. The results will be lower costs of production and less interference with individuals and firms choosing the best contractual pension arrangements to suit their individual and corporate needs.

A centerpiece of the less-regulated environment is the availability of unlimited individual retirement accounts (IRAs), subject to the same payout limits on tax-favored pension benefits during retirement as those now in place. Availability of IRAs creates competition between financial intermediaries and corporations to devise the best pension savings vehicles for workers. Once freed of unnecessary and costly regulation, firm-offered pension plans will survive only if they effect large productivity gains over alternative forms of compensation.

Pursuit of a neutral government policy towards pensions and retirement is not necessarily at odds with the need to raise tax revenue. A policy designed to reduce government influence over savings and retirement decisions will likely increase federal tax revenues—by significant amounts. In other words, some tax provisions impose economic costs on society and reduce revenue. Instead of interfering in arbitrary ways with pension funding decisions—which imposes additional layers of distortion—Congress could alter existing tax provisions that currently distort individual choice and, at the same time, raise large amounts of tax revenue. Pension funding at the corporate level still can be controlled by using methods that are more neutral in their impact on firms' and workers' choices of pensions and asset allocation in the pension trust.

A central theme of this book is that tax policy cannot be viewed in a vacuum; it is part of an overall national policy towards retirement income. A centerpiece of tax policy has always been the award of "special" treatment of savings for retirement consumption. This policy of special treatment recognizes the importance of not artificially increasing the cost of retirement through the tax system. But the tax code also has been congested with auxiliary regulatory provisions either to control the amount of revenue lost through the pension provisions or to effect other national retirement goals directed towards income redistribution and forced savings. As a result, a rather large regulatory framework has become intertwined with the tax policy itself.

Since the establishment of this regulatory framework, a generous and nearly universal social security system has emerged, which satisfies many of these goals; and modern computer technology makes it possible to directly control the size of pension incomes on an individual basis. These changes provide the opportunity for public policymakers to concentrate more on freeing individual decisions from unnecessary influence on both the public and private pension retirement systems, and to do so without reducing federal tax revenue or compromising the social goals embedded in the original set of rules.

THE ECONOMICS OF PENSIONS

As a prelude to evaluating tax policy, we need understand how pension plans work, how tax policy is translated into pension savings vehicles in the firm, and how these vehicles affect long-term relations between workers and firms. Later in the chapter, I will illustrate the impact of pension tax policy on the "price" of retirement and give some idea of the magnitude of the implications of altering this policy. These subjects will provide the framework for understanding and evaluating national pension and retirement policies that will be discussed in later chapters.

Defined Benefit versus Defined Contribution Plans

There are two basic types of pension plans: defined contribution and defined benefit. In a *defined contribution plan*, the firm deposits a fixed amount (often a percent of pay) into individual accounts for workers. By law, the worker usually vests in the account after no more than five years of participation.[4] After vesting, the workers own the accounts even if they quit the firm. If the workers stay until retirement, the entire value of the account is available to them, frequently as a lump sum.[5]

In a defined contribution plan, the firm is responsible for making required contributions, but is not responsible for ultimate benefit levels. For any given level of contributions, the pension benefit depends on investment experience in the fund. Investment risk is borne by participants. Subject to maximum contribution limits ($30,000 per year), all contributions by the firm are tax-deductible at the corporate level; and earnings are tax exempt during the accumulation period.

Defined contribution plans are the primary coverage for approximately 30 percent of pension-covered workers. In addition, more than half of all participants in defined benefit plans have a secondary defined contribution plan.

Most pension-covered workers are participants in a *defined benefit plan*. This type of plan promises an annuity commencing at retirement, usually based on final wages and service with the firm. The firm is responsible for delivering the stated benefit and for making contributions that reflect these promises. Contributions are tax deductible at the corporate level, and earnings are tax exempt during the accumulation period.

In defined benefit plans, workers do not have claims against individual accounts. Though, by law, accrued benefits vest after five years, workers may forgo a large proportion of their accrued benefits in real terms either if they leave the firm or if the firm fails prior to the attainment of normal retirement age.[6]

Since there is not an obvious one-to-one relationship between the pension promise and contributions as in defined contribution plans, the Internal Revenue Code sets rules to constrain the amount of contributions to defined benefit plans to prevent firms from abusing the tax-free accumulation vehicle.[7] As I will show below, the tax rules surrounding these pensions are more complex than those for defined contribution plans. Yet, at some fundamental level, the funding processes share great similarity.

In the next two sections, I will first demonstrate the similarities and differences in the funding procedures in both types of plans. Second, I will discuss the economic roles that distinguish defined benefit plans from defined contribution plans.

Funding Pension Plans

Consider two similar pension plans, one defined contribution, the other defined benefit. Both have the same retirement age, entail the same expected contribution levels, pay identical benefits at the same retirement age, and invest entirely in essentially risk-free Treasury bills (T-bills).

To illustrate simply, suppose there is only one worker in each plan, and he or she starts work at age 40. The chances of this worker quitting, being laid off, or dying prior to age 65 (retirement age) are presumed to be zero. The worker's cash wage is $10 per year. Assume that the inflation, interest, and expected wage growth rate are each 10 percent per year; thus, the real interest rate and real wage growth rate each is zero.

Defined contribution plan. In a defined contribution plan, suppose the firm promises to contribute 10 percent of the worker's wage to the defined contribution account. In our example, since real wages are $10 each year, 10 percent amounts to a contribution equal to one dollar per year in real terms (in nominal terms, contributions will increase because they are expressed as a percentage of nominal wages).

Each contribution will accumulate at a tax-free rate of return until retirement. Since the pension account invests solely in T-bills, which earn a zero real rate of return, the balance at the end of 25 years will be $25 in real terms.

Defined benefit plan. Now consider how this same benefit is provided in a defined benefit plan. First, I will discuss the funding rules that prevailed prior to the Omnibus Budget Reconciliation Act of 1987 (OBRA). This discussion will make the illustration of the basic funding pattern of defined benefit plans easier and will postpone, until a later chapter, the question of how and why OBRA increased the cost of providing defined benefit plans compared to the defined contribution alternative.

The firm starts by recognizing that it has promised the worker some defined benefit at retirement age. Even though defined benefit plans usually pay benefits in the form of an annuity, I will suppose for simplicity that the defined benefit plan in my example promises to pay the worker a lump sum equal to 10 percent, times final wage, times years of service. The expected present value of this benefit evaluated at the worker's current age (40) is $25, the same as in the defined contribution plan.

This amount is calculated as follows. Salary is assumed to increase with inflation, which, in the example, is assumed to be 10 percent per year; thus, the expected nominal wage at retirement will be $121.80 per year, not $10 as it is at age 40. The worker will also have 25 years of service at retirement. Thus, the lump-sum benefit is expected to be $304.56 (121.80 × 25 years service × 10%). Discounting this amount to the worker's current age (i.e., 40) at the 10 percent interest rate[8] amounts to $25. The pre-OBRA rules permitted the firm to contribute amounts to the pension trust in proportion to service accrued under the plan. In the example, the firm could deposit one dollar per year (in real terms) during each of the 25 years of service.[9,10]

Figure 1–1 depicts the growth of the trust fund in real dollars. Under the pre-OBRA funding rules, assuming a risk-free portfolio that yields a zero real rate of return, the fund is a linear schedule starting at zero, reaching $25 in 25 years; it increases at the rate of one dollar per year (also shown in the figure). These amounts are the same as those in a parallel defined contribution plan that makes the same $1 contribution (in real terms) during each of 25 years, amounting to $25 at age 65.

This simple example illustrates that, mechanically, defined benefit and defined contribution plans work in very different ways, but the essential economics of the funding procedures are similar. In reality, the defined benefit plan becomes more complex. For example, if the plan invests in stocks instead of T-bills, it may experience large invest-

FIGURE 1–1 Accumulation of Pension Benefits

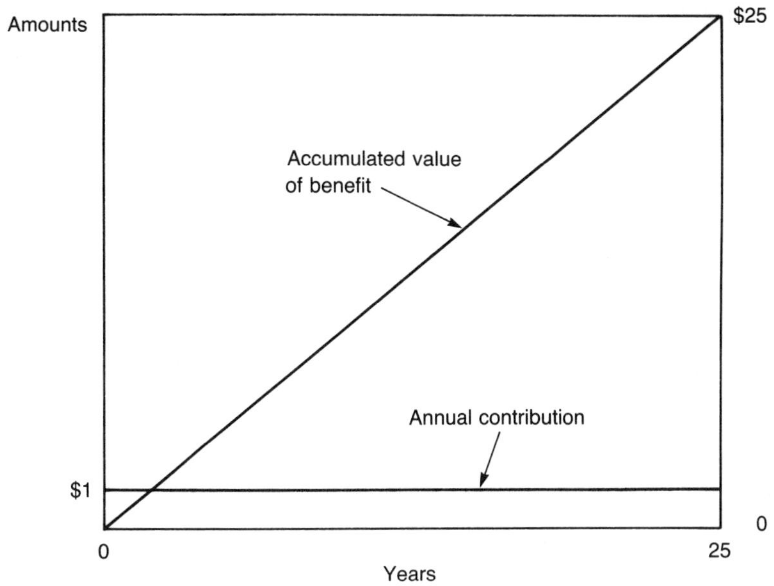

ment gains or losses. If so, this experience must be *amortized* in the form of lower or higher contributions over some period. I will delve further into these matters in a later chapter.

Advantages of Defined Benefit Plans

We need to recognize that defined contribution and defined benefit plans are not perfect substitutes. Some special value may be attached to defined benefit plans by workers and firms. Thus, if the government distorts the choice between these plans, an economic consequence will result. In this next section, as a prelude to policy discussions later in this book, I will discuss some of the special attributes of defined benefit plans.

Annuities. One advantage of defined benefit plans to *workers* is that these plans usually promise annuities, not lump sums. Often, defined contribution plans provide lump sums as the basic benefit form and almost always provide lump sums as an election.[11] Workers trying to convert a lump sum from a defined contribution plan into an annuity contract at retirement encounter unfavorable conditions. First, workers often face higher cost factors because they are assessed load factors based on individual rather than group contracts. Second, they encounter so-called selection problems. Older individuals who purchase annuities typically have longer life expectancy than average. This self selection makes it more expensive for individuals with average life expectancies to purchase annuities. These problems translate to lower benefits for the same stream of contributions and returns available in defined benefit plans.

Sharing investment risk. Another advantage of defined benefit plans to *workers* is that, despite investment experience, benefit levels are set in proportion to service and wage levels at retirement age. In effect, the pension promise at retirement is indexed to wages. If workers stay with the firm until retirement age, and the firm remains financially viable, workers receive their indexed retirement benefit as promised.

Sponsors of defined contribution plans can protect participants against investment risks by investing in short-term Treasury bills. Unlike stocks, T-bills exhibit little volatility of real returns; and unlike long-term bonds, T-bills are not affected in any important way by changing inflationary expectations. The problem is that workers must accept low rates of return in these portfolios compared to, say, all stock portfolios.

For example, from 1925 to 1987, the average annualized real rate of return on one-year T-bills was only .4 percent. An all stock portfolio, though riskier, exhibited a real return of 6.3 percent per annum over the same period.[12] Thus, expressed in real terms, a one-dollar investment in T-bills each year over this period would have yielded a balance of $26.30 at the end of the period; the same stream of contributions to an all stock portfolio would have yielded a balance of $60.80. Pension benefits can be more than twice as high in an all stock portfolio.

In a defined benefit plan, the firm (i.e., the stockholders) can facilitate risk-sharing among worker cohorts. For example, suppose benefits are set on the assumption that an all stock portfolio will return 6.3 percent per year over all worker cohorts' careers with the firm. Then, for one particular retiree cohort, the actual return during his or her lifetime might be 4.3 percent; for another, 8.3 percent. As long as the average is 6.3 percent over a relatively short period, workers can effectively insure each other against some uncertainty in pension benefits. If investment returns for a series of retiree cohorts do not match expectations, then, to the extent that stockholders have longer horizons than workers, stockholders might be willing to finance the shortfall for some worker cohorts at minimal cost.[13] In contrast, in defined contribution plans, various cohorts of retirees that had the same stream of real contributions can receive dramatically different retirement benefits, depending on the rate of return experienced over their particular tenure.

Quit costs. Defined benefit plans also have advantages to *firms*. One advantage is that, in order to claim the full value of the promised

TABLE 1–1 Quit Costs From a Defined Benefit Plan

		Interest Rates		
Age	*Service*	*i* = 5%	*i* = 10%	*i* = 15%
		As a Percent of Annual Wage		
45	5	31.6	43.2	47.5
50	10	52.7	77.6	89.4
55	15	59.0	94.8	116.5
60	20	44.2	78.6	105.5

NOTE: Retirement age is 65. Wage growth equals the interest rate.

benefit, a worker must stay with the firm until retirement age. Therefore, the retirement benefit becomes a means by which the firm can encourage long tenure with the firm. Though vested, workers who quit the firm are entitled to a benefit proportional to their wage level *at the time they quit*, not to their wage at retirement.

For example, a worker who quits after 15 years is entitled to a benefit value equal to 10 percent, times 15 years of service, times the nominal wage at year 15 of his tenure ($44.81). This benefit equals $67.22, payable at age 65. If the worker instead stays with the firm, the $67.22 essentially is indexed to 10 percent expected wage growth, or $182.72 at age 65. Thus, by quitting midway in the career, the worker gives up his claim to two thirds of the real pension benefit based on service accumulated to date.

The amount of the benefit loss from quitting depends upon the interest rate and the age and service level of the worker who quits. Table 1–1 lists these costs for the example illustrated above for different points in the worker's tenure, using different interest-rate assumptions. The losses are expressed as a percentage of the annual wage.[14] Table 1–1 shows that the cost of quitting can be large. For example, if the worker in the example quits after 10 years of service, he or she forgos at least the equivalent of a half year of wages, with amounts ranging over 100 percent of the annual age for higher interest rates.[15]

The imposition of these losses helps explain why quit rates for workers covered by defined benefit plans typically are much lower than those not covered by pension plans.[16] In contrast, since all interest and earnings in defined contributions plans belong to the worker after vesting, there are no quit costs in these plans once vesting occurs.

Retirement incentives. In defined benefit plans, the firm can also encourage retirement among older workers in two ways. First, it can make pensions actuarially unfair after normal retirement. Consider our example again. When our hypothetical worker reaches age 65, he has 25 years of service, entitling him to a benefit of $25 (in real terms). This amount equals 10 percent, times 25 years service, times $10 in wages.

Instead of receiving a lump-sum benefit, suppose the retiree receives an annuity indexed to prices until death. If we assume death is certain at age 80, the generosity level in the example translates to an annuity of $.067 (in real terms) per year of service. Thus, if the worker retires at age 64, he is entitled to an annuity equal to $1.60, which is actuarially reduced to $1.50 to accommodate one more year of annuity collection.

If the individual works his 64th year, two things happen: First, the $1.50 annuity is actuarially adjusted to $1.60, so that the present value of the annuity is the same $24. That is, when the interest rate is zero, the present value of $1.60 per year over 15 years of retirement is $24. Second, the worker receives one more year of credited service in the formula, which increases the annuity by the factor 25/24; the total annuity based on 25 years of service is $1.67, which has a present value of $25 at retirement age 65.

In contrast, if the same worker retires past the "normal" retirement age (65 in this example), he still receives the additional service benefit. But the $1.67 annuity based on 25 years of service is *not* actuarially adjusted. The worker loses $1.67 of "free" pension income or 16.7 percent of the annual $10 wage, by working his 65th year.

In contrast, in defined contribution plans, since the lump-sum value of the account belongs to the worker, it cannot be eroded by the worker's decision to work past normal retirement age. Thus, defined contribution plans generally have no retirement incentives.[17]

The incentives provided by defined benefit plans to encourage workers to stay with the firm until normal retirement age, but to retire after reaching normal retirement age, presumably are important tools to help firms maintain productive work forces. If these controls were not important, firms would not impose arbitrary penalties on workers who leave the firm "too soon" or stay "too late." If pension rules constrain worker preferences, the firm must pay higher wages to compensate workers for their loss of freedom. Thus, a firm that imposed unnecessary restrictions on workers would be unable to compete in the labor market with other firms that offered contracts with lower wages and fewer constraints.

Figure 1–2 demonstrates the incentive effects in defined benefit plans to leave the firm "on time." The numbers replicate the so-called quit costs in the second column of Table 1–1 (the nominal interest rate is set at 10 percent). The incentive to leave the firm after age 65 (the assumed "normal" retirement age) corresponds to the numbers used in the previous paragraphs. In reality, firms often provide a range of ages for the worker to retire without imposing any important penalties. This range often includes ages 62 through 65 and sometimes ages 55 through 65.[18]

FIGURE 1–2 Pension Benefits Forfeited by Leaving Firm "Too Early" or "Too Late"

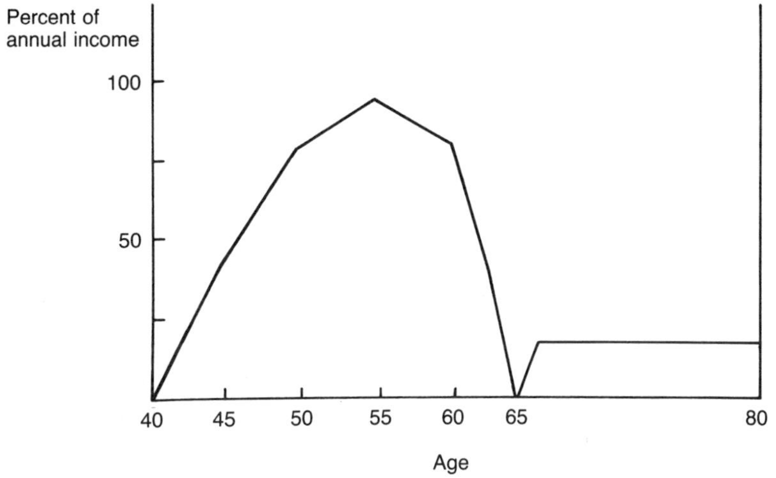

NOTES: Interest rate: 10%. Pension value: 10% of wage for each year of service.

Overall labor productivity. The incentive effects inherent in defined benefit plans can go beyond providing incentives to individual workers, particularly when workers are unionized. Where labor forces are unionized, there is a threat that the union could use its power to increase wages beyond competitive levels. Unions might exercise this power even if it ultimately leads to the financial failure of the firm, particularly if the work force is relatively old.

In these cases, defined benefit plans provide incentives for the union to help the firm remain financially viable over the long run. In these plans, if the firm fails, workers are entitled to *termination* benefits, not *ongoing* benefits. Termination benefits are exactly like benefits given to workers who quit the firm, and thus, to workers, entail large losses like those shown in the Table 1–1.[19] Thus, defined benefit plans provide unions with incentives to help the firm stay viable over the long run. Empirically, union workers are almost always covered by defined benefit plans, and have a much larger portion of wages in the form of pensions, which ensures large losses in the event of firm failure.[20]

In short, the advantages of defined benefit plans may work in both directions. Many firms and workers presumably attach significant value to these types of plans compared to defined contribution plans.

At the same time, while these plans are different, they share similar characteristics as devices to save monies for the purpose of providing pension benefits to workers when they reach retirement age.

Who Pays for the Pension?

Little progress can be made in developing a proper tax policy for pensions unless a fundamental aspect of pensions is understood. Pensions are not provided free: Workers must sacrifice cash wages in exchange for pension benefits. The easiest way to see this is to consider a defined contribution plan.

Suppose many identical firms compete in the same product and labor markets. Assume that all workers are equally productive and that there are no fringe benefits other than pensions. One firm pays a cash wage equal to $10 per year, plus a $1 contribution to a defined contribution plan. All other firms pay $10 in cash wages and give no pension. In this case, the first firm is paying compensation levels 10 percent higher than its competitors. Clearly, this situation is not stable.

Similarly, suppose all firms, except one, pay the wage plus pension described above. One firm, however, tries to reduce costs by paying only the $10 cash wage and providing no pension. This firm will have difficulty hiring workers because it pays a below-market level of compensation. Equilibrium occurs when all firms pay the same total compensation.

Though it is not as readily observable, the same principle applies to defined benefit plans. Here too, workers must pay for their pensions through forgone cash wages. The principle is easiest to see when workers are covered by unions (as are, roughly, one third of all workers in defined benefit plans). In these plans, unions usually negotiate a benefits package that explicitly represents trade-offs between cash wages and fringe benefits. Often, specific contribution rates are negotiated for the pension plans in lieu of some portion of cash wage.[21]

Even where the pension-wage trade off is not explicitly negotiated, the same economic logic makes the compelling argument that pensions are not provided gratis by firms: workers must pay for their pensions through lower cash wages. Otherwise, pension firms will not be able to compete effectively with nonpension firms.[22] The argument is not merely theoretical. A wealth of empirical evidence shows that workers pay for their fringe benefits through lower cash wages.[23]

Further, the evidence is consistent with the notion that implicit contributions through forgone wages for workers covered by defined benefit plans can be expressed as a constant percent of wages over all years with the firm.[24] In other words, the evidence suggests that workers covered by a defined benefit plan contribute in a pattern like that shown in Figure 1–1.

VALUE OF A TAX-EXEMPT TRUST ACCOUNT

The above discussion reminds us that, apart from some of the residual benefits of some types of pension plans, in essence, pension plans are vehicles that permit workers to save part of their earnings to support consumption during later years of their lifetimes, when their productive capacity is diminished and less certain. This simple fact would be more obvious if the federal government permitted individuals to have direct access to special trust-fund tax treatment to save for their own retirement.

Although individual retirement accounts (IRAs) are available, their contributions are limited to $2,000 per year, as compared with $30,000 in firm-offered defined contribution plans.[25] That the government essentially has mandated an intervening agent between workers and their retirement savings, however, does not alter the fundamental economics that lie behind pension plan accumulations: they represent worker savings for retirement. Obviously, the availability of special tax rules to pension savings is valuable.

Illustration of Tax Effects

In this section, I will construct some simple examples to illustrate the power of the tax-exempt status of pension trust funds. Except for limited concessions made to owner-occupied housing, the tax code does not offer tax-free accumulation vehicles for retirement savings outside the pension system.[26] For the sake of discussion, I will simply assume that on the margin, if pensions were not treated specially in the tax code, the alternative would be to save in tax-exposed vehicles.

Consider the simple case of a defined contribution plan. In lieu of some portion of cash wages, the firm contributes a fixed percent of the worker's earnings into a trust account; upon retirement, the worker receives a lump-sum amount. Compare this method of saving for retirement to one in which the individual saves for retirement outside the pension plan. In particular, consider a worker who faces a proportional income tax rate of 28 percent. Suppose this individual can choose whether the firm will either add $1 to the cash wage per year, which the worker will save outside the pension for retirement, or contribute $1 to a defined contribution plan.

Saving outside the pension plan. If the worker does not use the pension plan, the $1 "extra" wage is assessed a 28 percent personal income tax, leaving $0.72 free to save. Suppose the interest rate is 10 percent and the worker's tenure is 10 years prior to retirement. The $0.72 will not grow at the rate of 10 percent because savings outside the pension program are subject to the personal income tax. Thus, the after-tax interest rate is 7.2 percent (10 percent, minus the 28 percent

TABLE 1–2 Benefits of Tax-Free Accumulation

	Marginal Tax Rate	
Interest Rate	*15%*	*28%*
5	8.3	15.6
10	16.6	28.0
15	23.5	38.0

NOTE: Numbers in table denote the portion of after-tax pension income attributable to special pension tax policy. The example assumes a contribution rate equal to $1 (in real terms) per year for 25 years, with continuous compounding.

tax assessment). After 10 years, the $0.72 savings are worth $1.47 in after-tax income. This case is denoted in Figure 1–3 by the schedule labeled "no pension," which originates at $0.72 and ends at $1.47 after 10 years.

Saving inside the pension plan. Now, suppose the pension plan is used. If the $1 is deposited in the pension plan, no immediate tax is assessed; instead the money is treated as taxable income at retirement. This deferment is *not* what affects the present value tax liability. The key pension tax provision is that during the accumulation period, interest earned on pension plan assets is tax exempt. Thus, the $1 increases at the gross-of-tax rate of 10 percent per year, not the after-tax rate of 7.2 percent. After 10 years, the $1 contribution is worth $2.71. This growth is depicted by the schedule labeled "pension" in Figure 1–3. When the worker retires, his lump sum is subject to the 28 percent tax. After the tax, $1.95 in after-tax income is available to the worker.

This tax treatment is equivalent to one that assessed a 28 percent tax on the $1 in wages at the time it was saved and exempted interest earnings on this amount from further taxation. This alternative is shown by the schedule labeled "pension equivalent" in the figure which yields the same $1.95 after-tax income as the pension vehicle. That is, $.72 invested at 10 percent is worth $1.95 after 10 years. Viewing the pension tax advantage in this way, we can see that the value of the pension does not arise because the income tax is escaped or deferred, but rather because earnings on these savings are exempt from the so-called second tax during the accumulation period.[27]

Comparison of results. Compare the two results. With a pension, the $1 "extra" wage at age 55 is worth $1.95 after tax at age 65; without a pension, the same $1 is worth $1.47 after tax. The difference of $.48 is attributable to the tax-exempt status afforded earnings in the pension plan. In this example, fully 24 percent ($.48/$1.95) of the after-tax

FIGURE 1–3 Tax Benefits of a Tax-Exempt Trust

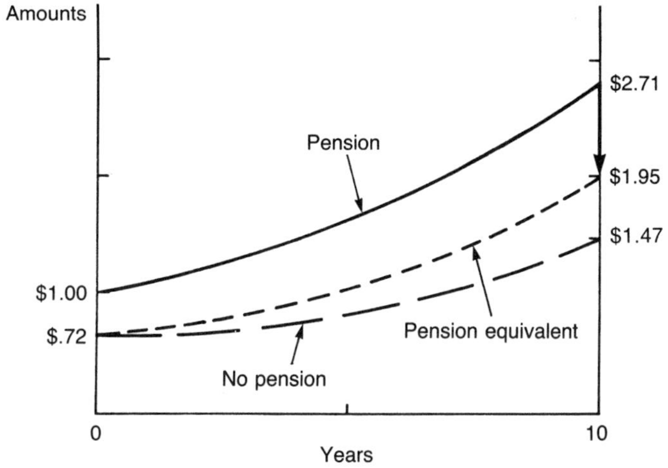

NOTE: Marginal tax rate: 28%; interest rate: 10%.

lump-sum pension will not be available to the worker if pension earnings do not have tax-exempt status.

The example can easily be generalized to the full work life. Reconsider the above example where workers maintain a constant pension savings rate over a 25-year period. The tax benefits attributable to tax-exempt accumulations for several interest rates and tax rates are reported in Table 1–2.[28]

The results show that the value of the tax exemption is substantial. In the case of the 15 percent tax rate and a 10 percent interest rate, 16.6 percent of after-tax pension income is attributable to the tax-exempt feature of pension earnings. The value increases with the interest rate and the marginal tax rate. For example, for an interest rate equal to 15 percent, the portion of after-tax pension income attributable to pension tax policy is 23.5 percent. At the 28 percent tax rate, these percentages are at least 50 percent higher.

In addition to the benefits attributable to tax-exempt accumulation in the pension trust, there also are some tax-smoothing advantages afforded pensions. I will consider this issue in the next chapter. For present purposes, it is sufficient to appreciate that even at the lower marginal tax rates enacted in the Tax Reform Act of 1986 (which are reflected in Table 1–2), the advantages of special income tax policy towards pension trust funds are substantial.

TABLE 1–3 Marginal Tax Rates and Pension Assets, 1920–1980

Year	*Personal Tax Rate (median taxpayer)*	*Income Tax Paid per 100 Workers*	*Pension Assets per Worker ($1980)*	*Corporate Tax Rate*
1920	4.0	13.3	$ 5	10.0
1930	1.1	4.2	69	12.0
1940	4.4	13.2	147	24.0
1950	17.4	59.7	349	42.0
1960	20.0	67.3	1,290	52.0
1970	19.0	69.8	2,423	49.2
1980	21.0	68.1	2,367	46.0

NOTE: Numbers in table are percents except where noted.

SOURCE: Richard Ippolito, *Pensions, Economics, and Public Policy* (Homewood IL: Dow Jones-Irwin, 1986), p. 25.

Implications for Pensions

The evidence suggests that the tax treatment of pensions is responsible for much of their growth. The data in Table 1–3 demonstrate this point. The data show the average marginal tax rates paid by taxpayers and the proportion of tax returns on which any tax was paid (see first two columns). In 1940, only 13 percent of income earners paid taxes, and these paid a median marginal tax rate equal to 4.4 percent. By 1950, 59.7 percent of income earners paid a tax with a median marginal tax rate equal to 17.4 percent. The dramatic increase in tax coverage and tax rates that took place during World War II were never reduced thereafter.

The data show that the ensuing decade marked a period of substantial growth for the U.S. pension system: per worker pension assets (in 1980 dollars) increased from $349 in 1950 to $1,290 in 1960 and to $2,423 in 1970. Pension asset growth after 1970 largely reflects a natural maturing process of pensions.[29] The time series data are therefore broadly consistent with the notion that income taxes could be substantially responsible for the growth of pensions as measured by per capita pension trust assets.[30]

The data in Table 1–4 summarize the current importance of pensions. In 1987, approximately nine million retirees were receiving benefits from private pension plans, amounting to $101 billion per year. Approximately two thirds of all private-sector workers are expected to retire with a pension worth on average about 23 percent of their final wage. In 1987, private pension funds held $1.6 trillion in assets and, together with state and local government pension funds, held over one fifth of all corporate equity securities and almost 40 percent of all corporate bonds. Clearly, pensions have grown to be an important institution in the United States.

TABLE 1–4 Pension Facts, 1987

Category	*Estimate*
Active participants (millions)	
Primary defined benefit	28.9
Primary defined contribution	11.6
Secondary plans	16.1
Total (includes double counts)	56.6
Coverage rate	
All ages	50%
Ages 50–54	65%
Pension amounts	
Initial annuity (annual)	$6,950
Replacement rate	23%
Total benefits paid (billions)	$101
Pension annuitants (millions)	
All retirees	9.0
First year retirees	515,000
Defined benefit plans	
Over 100 participants	25,000
Fewer than 100	200,000
Total	225,000
Defined contribution plans	
Over 100 participants	24,000
Fewer than 100	581,000
Total	605,000
Grand total	830,000
Pension assets (billions)*	
Defined benefit plans	$1,000
Defined contribution	600
Total	1,600
Share ownership*	
Corporate equity	23%
Corporate bonds	37%

NOTE: All data for private plans only except where denoted by an asterisk (*); these data include state and municipal public pension plans.

SOURCE: R. Ippolito, *Pensions, Economics and Public Policy*; and D. Beller and John Turner, *Trends in Pensions,* 1989.

SUMMARY

This chapter presents some of the basic economic issues surrounding pensions and pension tax policy. There are two types of pension plans: defined contribution and defined benefit. The former plans, which are the primary plans for approximately three out of ten workers covered by pensions, are straightforward tax-preferred savings accounts. Defined benefit plans tend to be more complex, perhaps providing important contributions to firms' productivity and important special benefits to workers.

Notwithstanding these issues, in their essence, pensions are means for workers to set aside some portion of their earnings during their more productive years to finance consumption during periods later in their lifetimes when their productive capacities are less certain. Even though the federal tax code essentially requires workers to set aside these savings through firm-offered pension plans instead of, say, individual retirement accounts with the same maximum contribution limits as defined contribution plans, this requirement should not obfuscate the essential fact that workers pay for their pensions, regardless of which vehicles are used to accumulate their savings. While admittedly oversimplifying the process, as a first-order approximation, the evidence suggests that workers finance their pensions by sacrificing some constant fraction of their annual compensation.

There is little dispute that the tax-exempt status afforded pension plan trusts is important. If it were not for special tax treatment, it is likely that after-tax pension annuities would be 15 to 30 percent lower, depending on the individual's tax rate and the prevailing long-term interest rate. The public policy question is whether federal tax policy ought to treat these savings specially in the tax code. This is the subject of the next chapter.

ENDNOTES

1. The second tax is assessed by including interest earned on savings as ordinary income. For the most part, interest merely reflects an adjustment for expected inflation, though there usually is a real interest rate component as well.
2. See Congressional Budget Office, *Tax Policy for Pensions and Other Retirement Saving* (Washington, D.C.: G.P.O., 1987), p. 14.
3. Most recently, the Omnibus Budget Reconciliation Act of 1987 imposed lower limits on permissible funding levels in defined benefit plans. See the discussion in Chapter 4.
4. If the plan provides for gradual instead of cliff vesting, full vesting can occur no more than seven years after participation begins.
5. See note 11.
6. If the firm fails, usually pensions are guaranteed by the Pension Benefit Guaranty Corporation, though these guarantees are much less than benefits available if the plan continued. See Richard A. Ippolito, *The Economics of Pension Insurance* (Homewood IL: Richard D. Irwin, 1989).
7. The Code also requires *minimum* contribution levels to ensure that at least some portion of promised benefits are funded in the pension trust fund.
8. This is the rate that is expected to be earned in the all T-bill portfolio chosen by the firm in the example.
9. In reality, there are several funding methods available to actuaries. The one described in the text corresponds to the so-called entry age-normal method which generates proportional funding on an ongoing basis. An alternative, for example, is the unit-credit method which permits firms to underfund their plans on an ongoing basis until the worker approaches normal retirement age. See E. Allen et al., *Pension Planning* (Homewood, IL: Richard D. Irwin, 1989).
10. In year one, for example, corresponding to age 40, the worker's first year of service, the firm's ongoing liability at the end of the year is $1 (10%, times current wage of $10, times one year of service, projected at the rate of wage growth of 10

percent per year to retirement age 65, discounted back to age 40 at the interest rate of 10 percent):

$$\text{PVO}(1,0) = 10\% \times 1 \text{ year} \times \$10e^{(.10-.10)25} = \$1, \tag{1–1}$$

where PVO(1,0) is the present value of the ongoing pension after one year of service, evaluated in year-zero dollars. This is exactly like its equal-value, identical-portfolio defined contribution counterpart: the sponsor of a defined benefit plan is permitted to deposit the same one dollar in contributions in year one.

Now consider year 15 of the worker's service. The wage then is expected to be $44.81 ($10 accumulated at 10 percent wage growth for 10 years); service is 15 years; and there are 10 years to retirement. Thus, according to equation 1–1, the ongoing benefit liability in year-15 dollars is:

$$\text{PVO}(15,15) = 10\% \times 15 \text{ years} \times \$44.81e^{(.10-.10)10} = \$67.22. \tag{1–2}$$

In year-15 dollars, the present value of the accumulated benefit is $67.22. In year-zero dollars, this amount is discounted 15 years at the 10 percent interest rate:

$$\text{PVO}(15,0) = \$67.22e^{-.10(15)} = \$15. \tag{1–3}$$

The firm's permitted contribution prior to the new OBRA rules equaled the difference between benefits at age 65 and current benefits, prorated over years left until retirement. Since, in real terms, the present value of benefits at age 65 is expected to be $25, the difference between this and benefits accrued at year fifteen ($15), spread over 10 years of remaining service is $1: therefore, the firm's normal contribution in year fifteen is $1 (valued in year-zero dollars).

11. While most defined contribution plans provide for the annuity option at retirement, rarely do they require participants to take the benefit in the form of annuities. An exception is TIAA-CREF. By enforcing a requirement to take the annuity-only form, a defined contribution plan can eliminate the adverse selection problem created by providing retirees a choice between a lump sum and an annuity form of payment.
12. See Ibbotson Associates, *Stocks, Bonds, Bills, and Inflation* (Chicago: Ibbotson Associates, 1988), p. 69.
13. If this return turns out to be unusually low for a succession of cohorts, or similarly, if the structural return falls from 6.3 percent to, say, 4.0 percent, it is less clear that stockholders will be willing to accept these risks without the benefit of the risk premia imbedded in stock returns. A more plausible explanation is that workers with riskier portfolios will expect high benefits on average, but will share in some of the downside risk if poor returns are experienced. While federal regulation of pensions restricts the amount of risk sharing that can occur (the firm must pay a flow equal to benefits accrued to date in nominal terms), the sharing could take other forms. For example, the firm could award lower ad hoc inflation adjustments during retirement.
14. As the worker ages and accrues more service, the portion of the accrued pension he forgoes first increases, then decreases. As the worker approaches retirement age, the amount of inflation erosion he suffers on his pension benefit if he quits is less than it would be if he quit at an earlier age. But, with more service, he accumulates more pension benefits which works in the direction of increasing quit losses at later ages. Thus, the loss function has a hill-like appearance with age.
15. In general, the pension plan illustrated is less generous than most plans. The typical lump sum equivalent for defined benefit plans has a generosity factor

closer to 15 percent, not 10 percent of final wage, times service. Thus, the quit costs in the table are roughly two thirds of the average. See David McCarthy, *Findings from the Survey of Private Pension Benefit Amounts* (Washington, D.C.: U.S. Department of Labor [G.P.O], 1985). Some pension plans can have quit costs two to three times those illustrated in the table. An example is the pension that covers most federal workers hired prior to 1983. See Richard Ippolito, "Why Federal Workers Don't Quit," *Journal of Human Resources* (Spring 1987), pp. 281–299.

16. See for example, Steven Allen et al., "Job Mobility, Older Workers, and the Role of Pensions" (Final Report submitted to the U.S. Department of Labor, 1986); Ann Bartel and George Borjas, "Middle-Age Job Mobility: Its Determinants and Consequences," in *Men in Their Pre-Retirement Years* (Philadelphia: Temple University School of Business Administration, 1977); Olivia Mitchell, "Fringe Benefits and Labor Mobility," *Journal of Human Resources* (Spring 1982), pp. 286–298; and Bradley Shiller and R. Weiss, "The Impact of Private Pensions on Firm Attachments,"*Review of Economics and Statistics* (1980), pp. 360–380.
17. The plan can, however, impose a limit on the number of years during which a contribution will be made; thus, contributions can stop after 25 or 30 years of service.
18. Sometimes, the formulas are skewed to offer some subsidy to early retirement—that is, the actuarial adjustment is less than complete. The Internal Revenue Code does not permit formulas to be less than actuarially fair for early retirees. It is important to understand, however, that actuarially equivalent pensions are not always economically equivalent. See Richard A. Ippolito, "Towards Explaining Earlier Retirement After 1970," *Industrial & Labor Relations Review* (1990), forthcoming.
19. If the failed firm has insufficient assets to pay termination benefits, most of these benefits are guaranteed by the government pension insurance company.
20. Even though defined contribution plans can take the form of profit-sharing plans or stock-bonus plans, neither can replicate the loss function imparted by a terminated defined benefit plan. See Richard A. Ippolito, *Pensions, Economics, and Public Policy* (Homewood, IL: Dow Jones-Irwin, 1986), Chapter 10.
21. This is the case, for example, in so-called multiemployer plans.
22. Even if pensions increase productivity, this does not imply that workers receive all the benefits: workers will receive higher wages only to the extent that a higher wage is necessary to compensate them for some constraints on their freedom that might be imposed by defined benefit plans. There is only one competitive wage level (adjusting for labor skills). Firms must pay this wage regardless of productivity levels in the firm. If firms pay too little, they are unable to retain labor. If they pay too much, they are unable to compete in product markets. If pensions increase productivity, competition among firms ensure that, for the most part, these improvements in productivity translate into lower prices, not higher wages in the firm. If these gains are important across lots of firms, workers as a whole receive the benefits through higher real wages.
23. See Ronald Ehrenberg, "Retirement System Characteristics and Compensating Wage Differentials in the Public Sector," *Industrial & Labor Relations Review* (1980), pp. 470–483; Bradley Schiller and R. Weiss, "Pensions and Wages: A Test for Equalizing Differences," *Review of Economics and Statistics* (1980), pp. 529–538; and Robert S. Smith, "Compensating Differentials for Pensions and Underfunding in the Public Sector," *Review of Economics and Statistics* (1981), pp. 463–468. A good textbook on the issues of compensating differentials in wages is Ronald Ehrenberg and Robert Smith, *Modern Labor Economics* (Glendale, IL: Scott Foresman, 1985).

24. See Robert Clark and Ann McDermed, "Life Cycle Patterns of Earnings, Pension Wealth, and Total Compensation," *Quarterly Journal of Economics* (1986), pp. 341–362, and also their paper "Earnings Response to Pension Coverage and Eligibility" (Paper presented at the American Economic Association Meetings, New York, 1985); Christopher Cornwell et al., "Opportunistic Behavior by Firms in Implicit Pension Contracts" (Mimeograph, West Virginia University, 1988); Richard A. Ippolito, "The Labor Contract and True Economic Pension Liabilities," *American Economic Review* (December 1985), pp. 1031–1043; and Olivia Mitchell and S. Pozzenbon, "Wages, Pensions, and the Wage-Pension Trade-off" (Paper presented at the American Economic Association Meetings, New Orleans, 1986).

25. Self-employed individuals are entitled to set up so-called Keough plans, but these plans limit contributions to $7,000 per year.

26. Most tax consessions in the code are arbitraged. Thus, investors in tax-exempt municipal bonds do not generally expect a yield in excess of the after-tax yield available on taxable bonds. The same arbitrage would occur in housing except for the stipulation in the tax code that the exemption from taxation on sales proceeds of owner-occupied housing for homeowners after age 55 is limited to $125,000 per household. Up to this amount, tax treatment of earnings devoted to purchasing a house is the same as pensions in the sense that they are taxed only once. The difference is in timing of the tax assessment: pension contributions are exempt from taxation and, instead, are taxed as benefits at retirement. Housing investments are taxed as ordinary income, but proceeds up to $125,000 are exempt from taxation for homeowners after age 55. The present value tax liabilities are the same up to this amount. To the extent that pension-covered workers do not fully exploit the housing-tax loophole then part of the tax advantage afforded pensions can be preserved by investing more in the form of housing.

27. When the tax rate is not the same during retirement and work years, an additional tax effect occurs. I will deal with this issue in Chapter 2.

28. Suppose contributions to the pension plan are $1 in the first year of tenure and increase at the rate of g percent (reflecting inflation and real wage growth). If this savings flow is deposited in conventional vehicles, the savings is subject to normal income taxation before it is deposited, then is assessed on the interest earned in each period. Hence, the after-tax balance after R years of accumulation is

$$B = (1 - t)\int_{j=0}^{R} e^{gj + (1-t)i(R-j)}dj,$$

where i is the interest rate and t is the proportional tax rate. If the pension is used instead, the tax rate t inside the integral is set equal to zero. The tax factor $(1 - t)$ outside the integral remains because pension payouts are subject to taxation. Denote this solution by the variable P. The portion of after-tax pension income attributable to the tax-exempt status of pensions is $(P - B)/P$.

29. It takes upwards of 50 years for all retiree ages to become filled with succeeding cohorts of retirees and for retiring workers to benefit from an entire career under a pension plan. See R. Ippolito, *Pensions, Economics, and Public Policy*, Chapter 5.

30. This does not imply that pension plans were nonexistent prior to 1940. See Murray Latimar, *Industrial Pension Systems* (New York: Industrial Relations Counselors, 1932).

CHAPTER 2

Economic Justification of Pension Tax Policy

Why should the government award special tax-exempt status to pension trust funds? The defense of the system does not lie in the government trying to encourage early retirement or higher levels of consumption during retirement. Quite the opposite is true. Its defense is that the policy avoids application of a *double tax* on retirement savings. In effect, as will be shown below, the policy gets the government out of the business of influencing retirement decisions, leaving these matters to individual choice.

Put another way, the special tax treatment restricts the effective tax rate on income used for retirement consumption to the marginal rate stated in the Internal Revenue Code; without these rules, the statutory rates are increased substantially, but *only* if income is used to support consumption later in life.

ECONOMIC EFFICIENCY AND DISTORTIONS

It is useful to start by introducing a framework to evaluate the impact of public policy on an otherwise free market. For the sake of illustration, consider the market for fish depicted in Figure 2–1, Part (a). The figure might depict pounds of fish consumed during some period of time, say one year. The demand curve slopes downward, reflecting diminishing marginal value to consumption.

That is to say, the first few fish meals that are consumed are highly valued, so consumers are willing to pay a relatively high price for these, say P_H. After they have consumed lots of fish during the year, they are willing to pay a lower price for incremental fish meals, say price P_L. The quantity of fish actually consumed during the year depends on demand *and* supply conditions.

FIGURE 2–1 Efficiency Concepts

Part (a): Description of a Free Market

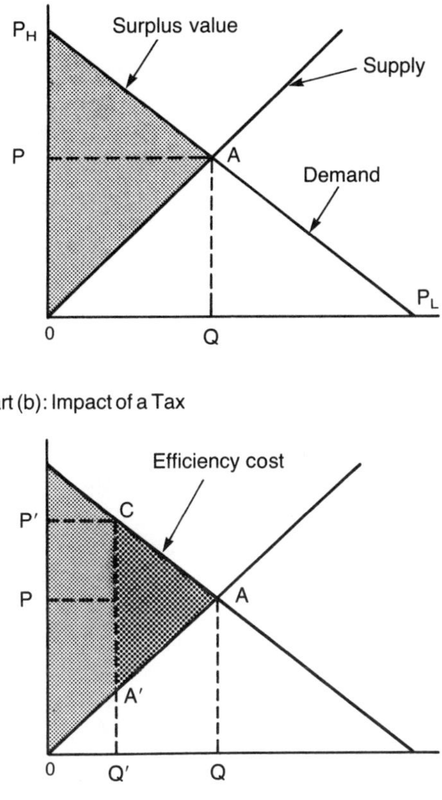

The amount of fish supplied is reflected in the upsloping schedule in the figure. At the low price P_L, fishermen might exploit some coastline schools of fish, which they can harvest at low cost. At the high price P_H, they might be willing to rent more boats, hire more labor, and harvest more distant, harder-to-find schools of fish. Equilibrium is determined when the marginal cost of finding and bringing to market one more pound of fish is equal to the marginal value of consuming one more pound of fish. In the figure, this equilibrium is described by the intersection of supply and demand, labelled point A. Market price is P and quantity of fish supplied and consumed is Q.

The value added from this market is described as follows: The total value of consuming Q pounds of fish is the summation of the marginal value of consuming each pound of fish from 0 to Q; this amount is described by the area under the demand curve, area $0P_HAQ$. The total cost of farming the fish and bringing them to market is equal to the area under the supply curve, area 0AQ. The difference between the total value of consumption and the total cost of supplying the quantity Q of fish represents "surplus" value, denoted by the shaded area $0P_HA$ in the figure.

Now suppose the government imposes a tax on fish consumption in the amount P–P′ per pound. The impact of this tax is depicted in Figure 2–1, Part (b). The tax has the effect of raising price to consumers from P to P′. At the higher price, consumers are willing to eat fewer pounds of fish. They will consume the amount of fish denoted by the amount Q′ in the figure rather than amount Q because further fish consumed beyond Q′ are valued less than the new price, including the tax. Thus, only Q′ fish are harvested and brought to market.

This tax has imposed a *distortion* on the fish market, because, in the absence of a tax, more resources would have been devoted to fishing, and more fish would have been consumed. This distortion results in *economic inefficiency* or, equivalently, *economic cost* because even though the incremental quantity of fish Q–Q′ can be brought to market at a cost less than the value attached to the fish by consumers, the fish, in fact, will not be marketed. They will not be marketed because the tax acts to make consumers act as though the marginal cost of production is P′, when in reality the economic cost is only P. The measure of this inefficiency is the difference between the value attached to the incremental fish no longer consumed and the cost that would have been incurred to supply the additional fish. The inefficiency is denoted by the blackened triangular area A′AC in Part (b) of the figure.

As a general rule, when the government interferes with the operation of a market, economic costs are imposed because the interference distorts the behavior of consumers and suppliers from the optimal production and consumption of goods, services, or methods of production.[1] This is the essential argument why government policy towards retirement decisions should be guided by the free market. If the government artificially distorts relative prices of retirement consumption through the tax system, individuals will react to the distorted price system just as participants in the fish market reacted in Figure 2–1 (compare parts *a* and *b* in the figure).

That is to say, if the price of retirement is artificially increased through government policy, workers will retire later and consume less during retirement, just as a tax on fish would lead to less production and consumption of fish and more production and consumption of, say meat. The distorted retirement equilibrium is inefficient, just as the fish market depicted in Figure 2–1, Part (b), because workers and consumers essentially are prevented from creating the combination of leisure and consumption over a lifetime that maximizes overall economic value.

ILLUSTRATION OF HIGHER INCOME TAX RATES ON FUTURE CONSUMPTION

With these ideas in mind, I will now proceed with a discussion of the impact of a hypothetical pension tax policy, one that does not award tax-free status to pension trust funds. Such a policy increases the relative cost of retirement which, in turn, causes distortions in workers' behavior and thus imposes economic cost on society.

To illustrate, consider a 40-year-old worker who pays a marginal income tax rate of 15 percent. Suppose the interest rate is 5 percent, and the real rate of interest is zero, so that the entire 5 percent interest reflects the anticipated rate of inflation. Thus, if $1.00 is saved for consumption next year, its value will increase with interest to $1.05, which will enable the individual to purchase the same commodity next year when it costs $1.05.

Suppose now that the age-40 individual wishes to postpone $1 of current wages to have available for consumption at age 65. Owing to inflation, which I assume amounts to 5 percent per year, products that cost $1.00 today will cost $3.49 in 25 years (one dollar compounded continuously at 5 percent per annum for 25 years is $3.49). The change in nominal prices is not a problem as long as my hypothetical saver can earn the full 5 percent interest rate. The worker's $1.00 also will increase with accumulated interest to $3.49 at age 65.

If the worker must save in a tax-exposed savings vehicle, however, $3.49 will not be available to spend in 25 years; that is, if the worker saves the $1 in a tax-exposed vehicle, he earns the *after-tax* interest rate. If the worker faces a tax rate of 15 percent, the after-tax interest rate is 4.25 percent, not 5 percent. Thus, at age 65, the worker has $2.89 available, only 82.9 percent of the $3.49 needed to purchase the same products that cost $1.00 at age 40.

In effect, there is an extra income tax applied to earnings *only if* these earnings are saved for future consumption. If the age-40 worker in the example consumes one dollar in earnings immediately, there is no extra tax. But if he saves the $1 for later consumption at age 65, in effect, his dollar is assessed an extra tax in an amount equal to 17.1 percent of the original $1 in savings.[2] Thus, because of the so-called double tax, the worker pays tax on earnings once, then pays a second tax (in a series of increments) as he tries to convert today's dollars into tomorrow's dollars. By waiting to spend $1 instead of consuming it immediately, the worker in the example loses 17.1 cents of that dollar's purchasing power.

Impact on effective income tax rate. It is useful to restate this extra tax as an addition to the stated income tax rate on earnings. The worker in the example faces an income tax rate statutorily set at 15 percent. Thus, our hypothetical worker presumably started out earning approximately $1.18 in gross earnings; then he was assessed an income tax at the rate of 15 percent, leaving $1 in after-tax earnings.

If this worker spends the $1 immediately, the statutory income tax on the original $1.18 wage is 15 percent. But if the worker postpones consumption until age 65, the $1.18 wage is assessed a double tax: First, a 15 percent income tax is assessed, leaving $1 after tax. Then, several additional income tax assessments are made on the interest earned as the worker tries to translate today's dollars into tomorrow's dollars. These additional tax assessments amount to 17.1 percent of the amount saved, leaving 82.7 cents in real terms to spend at age 65.[3] Thus, the *total* income tax assessed on our hypothetical worker's earnings is not 15 percent, but almost 30 percent.

In effect, the statutory income tax rate is higher than stated in the Internal Revenue Code, *but only if earnings are used to support later consumption.* The extra tax rate is higher, if there is a higher rate of interest, a longer savings period, or a higher marginal tax rate. These effective income tax rates are shown in Table 2–1 for individuals aged 30 through 60, for interest rates equal to 5 and 10 percent and for individuals facing statutory marginal tax rates of 15 and 28 percent. Future consumption occurs at age 65.

The table makes it clear that income tax rates on earnings used for later consumption greatly exceed those stated in the Internal Revenue Code. When the interest rate is 10 percent, an age-40 worker pays a 28 percent marginal tax rate on earnings used to support immediate consumption and a 64.2 percent tax rate on earnings used to support age-65 consumption.

The net effect of "special" pension tax policy is to reestablish the income tax rates announced in the Internal Revenue Code, regardless of whether earnings are used to support immediate or future consumption. In so doing, a large distortion against savings for retirement is removed. In my hypothetical example (interest rate equals 5 percent; marginal tax rate equals 15 percent), the age-40 worker is entitled to save the original $1.18 in earnings in the pension trust, which will earn the full pre-tax interest rate of 5 percent, leaving a balance of $4.10 at age 65. After paying the 15 percent income tax on the pension distribution, the worker is left with $3.49 to spend at age 65, which is worth exactly $1.00 in real terms.[4]

Impact on federal tax revenue. These arguments demonstrate why it is misleading to label special tax treatment of pensions as a tax "expenditure." The special tax treatment of pensions merely prevents the U.S. Treasury from levying a higher income tax rate than is statu-

TABLE 2–1 Tax Rates on Immediate versus Future Consumption

Age Income Is Earned	*Tax Rate on Consumption at Age 65*	
	i = 5%	*i = 10%*
	Statutory Tax Rate: 15%	
40	29.5	41.6
50	24.0	32.1
60	18.1	21.1
	Statutory Tax Rate: 28%	
40	49.2	64.2
50	41.6	52.6
60	32.8	37.4

NOTE: Numbers in the table are percents.

torily provided against wage income when it is used to support retirement consumption.

The amount of tax revenue that otherwise might be collected, except for the pension provision in the code, can be calculated if the assumption is made that individuals' behavior is unaffected by a tax code that exposes pension trust funds to taxation. Table 1–2 in Chapter 1 suggests that if the long-term interest rate is 10 percent, individuals will collect after-tax pensions that are 16.6 and 28 percent less if earnings are subject to taxation, the amounts depending on whether workers' tax rates are 15 or 28 percent. Expressed as a percent of before-tax pension benefits, these numbers are 14.1 and 20.1.

Assuming that workers are spread between these tax rates in the ratio of 1:1[5], the average portion of before-tax pension income that has been collected in the form of an extra tax levy is 17 percent. Annual private pension benefits in 1989 are in the range of $110 billion per year.[6] Thus, on the assumption that there are no income-smoothing effects from pensions (see next section), then elimination of special tax-exempt status to pensions would generate additional tax revenue in the amount of $19 billion per year. If state and local government pensions were added to this, the amount would be closer to $25 billion.[7,8]

INCOME SMOOTHING EFFECTS

Thus far, I have ignored a second income tax advantage from pensions: that is, their tendency to smooth taxable income over the lifetime. In a proportional tax system with no deductions, income smoothing has no implications for lifetime taxes. In a progressive income tax system, however, income smoothing has the effect of *reducing* the statutory income tax rates set out in the Internal Revenue Code. This produces a distortion in the opposite direction to the double tax on workers' decisions to retire.

For example, consider a worker paying a 28 percent marginal income tax rate. If he spends one dollar of earnings immediately, he keeps 72 cents. If he saves the dollar through a pension fund to consume during retirement, he may pay a lower marginal tax rate, say 15 percent. If this is so, the worker keeps 85 cents out of his one dollar in earnings. Postponed consumption is taxed more lightly than immediate consumption.

The Tax Reform Act of 1986 eliminated the income tax smoothing effects for a significant portion of taxpayers because it established two broad marginal tax rates at the 15 and 28 percent levels.[9] Thus, to the extent that workers remain in the same tax bracket during work and retirement, the smoothing effect is eliminated. A back-of-the-envelope calculation suggests that approximately half of all households still might benefit from the income-smoothing effect of pensions.[10] For these individuals, the effect is worth up to 15 cents on each dollar of pension income taxed at a lower rate during retirement. This artifact of the tax code will artificially encourage these workers to prefer future consumption to current consumption and thus will encourage premature retirement.

The smoothing effect can be eliminated for all workers, thereby removing a distortion favoring spending during retirement. This correction can be made by changing the tax code to require all reported pension income to be taxed in full[11] at the same marginal tax rates paid during work years. This change would raise tax revenue and remove one of the remaining tax distortions affiliated with the pension system.[12] An equally effective alternative is to subject all pension contributions to taxation during the individual's worklife and exempt all pension income from taxation during retirement. As discussed in Chapter 1, this is economically equivalent to current pension tax policy, except that it eliminates the income-smoothing effect (see, in particular, Figure 1–1).[13]

A rough measure of the current impact of such a change can be derived by a back-of-the-envelope calculation. Suppose that half of all workers receiving pensions are able to shift to a lower marginal tax bracket compared to what they had during their work years. For simplicity, assume that all of their pension incomes are taxed at the lower bracket during retirement. Annual private pension payouts in 1989 were roughly $110 billion per year. The typical income-smoothing effect for those affected by smoothing is approximately 15 percent (the difference in tax rates during work and retirement years). This means that long-run revenues from this change in policy might be higher in the amount of $8.25 billion per year for private-sector workers ($110 billion, times the 15 percent tax effect, times 50% of workers affected).

Remember that, at existing tax rates, the tax-exempt pension trust fund provision reduces tax revenue by approximately $19 billion per year (in 1989 dollars). Adding the income-smoothing effect increases this number to almost $27 billion ($35 billion including government workers). What the above argument suggests is that Congress could recapture approximately 25 percent of this loss by eliminating the income-smoothing effect and, in so doing, increase economic efficiency.

Social security income. There is a parallel income tax distortion inherent in the social security system. Currently, half of social security contributions are subject to the individual income tax during work years (the so-called individual's contribution). The other half, though technically the "employer's contribution," is exactly like an "employer contribution" to a pension plan. Both, in effect, are a part of wages; and, presumably, workers effectively pay for both pensions and social security through lower cash wages.

From the perspective of efficient tax policy, the problem with social security is that this "second half" of the contribution is *never* subject to taxation. Thus, there is an explicit distortion in the federal income tax code, encouraging overuse of the social security system: that is, workers are encouraged to overvalue social security, not because the system itself is valuable, but because there is a hidden tax subsidy embedded in the system.

This distortion was partially addressed in the Social Security Amendments Act of 1983. The second half of social security income was included as taxable income, but only for individuals with taxable income in excess of $25,000 and for couples with taxable income in excess of $32,000. (The tax revenue raised by this provision is transferred to the social security trust fund.) If social security is put on the same tax basis as private pensions, these limits would have to be eliminated. In this way, all social security income would be taxed once (half when contributions were made, and half when benefits were received). This is analytically equivalent to taxing all social security income at the time benefits are collected, just like private pensions.

Actually, these limits will effectively be eliminated over the long run. The 1983 amendments were written specifically to freeze the $25,000 and $32,000 thresholds at these *nominal* levels. Over the long run, as inflation takes its inevitable toll, the real value of the thresholds will gradually fall towards zero. Thus, for example, if the inflation rate was 5 percent per annum, after 20 years these limits would be more like $10,000 and $12,000 in real terms. There is some reason to believe that the thresholds will not be adjusted upwards in future years.[14] If this policy, in fact, is carried out as intended, then a neutral tax policy towards social security benefits will be effected, albeit over a long period of time.[15]

If the income tax smoothing effect is eliminated for private pensions, it should be eliminated for social security. All pensions and half of all social security income should be taxed separately at rates that reflect marginal tax rates during work years. Since low-income individuals would pay no income tax during work years, there would be an automatic exemption of the tax for these individuals.

To give some idea of the revenue impact from this source, consider that social security benefits paid to retired workers in 1986 was $124 billion.[16] In the long run, half of these benefits, or $62 billion, will be subject to the income tax. Then, using the same rules of thumb as above (50 percent of households will benefit from income smoothing, and the amount of the tax benefit will be 15 percent of benefits received), an additional $4.6 billion in tax revenue can be raised annually ($62 billion, times 50 percent of recipients, times 15 percent income-smoothing benefit). In 1989 dollars, the revenue impact of this change in policy would exceed $5 billion.

Again, these adjustments to the tax code represent opportunities to raise revenue and, at the same time, remove the government from the business of influencing retirement decisions through the tax system. Since individuals have retired under the expectation of existing rules, however, the introduction of these new rules should be phased in over a lengthy period.

IMPACT OF ELIMINATING SPECIAL PENSION TAX POLICY

Given the tax structure in the United States, pensions are an efficient way to save income to support consumption during retirement years. Retirement does not usually occur because workers are no longer a productive part of the work force. Most workers—who typically enjoy better health and longer life expectancies than their predecessors who retired at older ages[17]—could work productively for many years beyond their age of retirement (which most typically occurs in the workers' early 60s).[18]

Viewed broadly, retirement is a choice variable for workers. Retirement is a bunching of leisure at the end of life. If wages were sufficiently low, workers simply could not afford to take this amount of leisure.

Similarly, if government policy made it prohibitively costly to save for retirement, workers would choose less of it. In this sense, federal tax policy toward the accumulation of worker savings for retirement undoubtedly will influence the broad scheme of observed retirement practices. Within this framework, it is interesting to try to predict the likely impact of eliminating the tax-exempt status of pension plan trust funds.

Retirement Age and Consumption

For the purposes of this discussion, I will assume that the income-smoothing effect will be eliminated in future tax legislation, so that what remains is the tax-exempt status of pension trust funds.

Without pensions, savings for retirement will be costly, and hence workers generally will retire later and enjoy lower standards of living during retirement. This point is made in Table 2–1, which shows that in the absence of the tax-exemption granted pension trust funds, the effective tax levied against income earned and saved for future consumption is much higher than tax rates levied against income used to finance immediate consumption. To illustrate how workers might react to a tax code policy that eliminated the tax-exempt pension fund status, I will consider a simple example.

Consider a worker who saves for retirement without a pension. This person earns $10 in real terms per year from age 35 until age 65 and, with certainty, will die at age 80. Suppose the expected inflation rate is 5.5 percent, and the real interest rate is 2 percent, so that the nominal long-term interest rate is 7.5 percent. Also, suppose for convenience that the prevailing tax rate is precisely 26.6 percent. In this case, the worker's after-tax real interest rate is zero.[19] All consumption and savings numbers in the example will be stated in real terms.

The worker intends to enjoy a constant level of income over his 45-year life after age 35. The worker would like to consume $6.66 per year ($10 × 30 years of work divided by 45 years of consumption). This means that a total of $100 is needed to support years of retirement after age 65 (i.e., $100/15 = $6.66). If the worker does not have access to a pension, he can earn an after-tax real rate of return, which, in this example, is zero. Thus, to support retirement in the amount of $100 in real terms, the worker must sacrifice $3.33 of consumption each year during the work life.[20]

This situation changes with a pension. Since pension earnings are tax exempt, the worker can earn a pre-tax real interest rate (2 percent in the example) on the savings made each year to support retirement. This means he can support the identical retirement consumption level of $100 by saving only $2.43 per year.[21] Thus, by using the pension, the individual consumes $.90 (= $3.33 − $2.43), or 13.5 percent more during work years without reducing retirement consumption.[22]

If the worker without a pension wants to save the same $2.43 per year instead of $3.33 and maintain consumption at the level of $6.66 per year, he can work three more years, retiring at age 68 instead of 65.[23] *Thus, one way workers can reduce the impact of taxation on interest income is to take fewer years of retirement*—hence reducing the need to transfer monies through savings that trigger the extra tax assessments.

On the other hand, *workers can reduce the level of consumption during retirement* and maintain the retirement age of 65. This option is accomplished by reducing retirement consumption from $6.66 per year to $4.86.[24]

Also, *workers can switch leisure away from older to younger ages.* In the extreme, if all workers remained fully productive until death, they could take the same amount of lifetime leisure by working shorter work weeks and never retiring. In this way, lifetime consumption and lifetime leisure would be the same as under the current pension tax policy; it simply would be rearranged.[25] For example, if the worker in the example reduced his work week by one third, he could earn $6.67 per year over 45 years with no retirement. There would be no savings and thus no "extra" tax levies on interest earnings. Of course, if workers lose productivity as they age and/or firms are less efficient if workers work shorter work weeks, this "rearrangement" of leisure could have important implications for productivity (and thus wages).

In short, if tax-preferred status for pensions was eliminated (their tax-exempt status canceled), an additional tax burden would be imposed on early retirement and retirement consumption. Rather than react in only one of the ways described above, workers more likely will react in some combination. They likely will retire at later ages, enjoy lower standards of living during retirement, and work shorter work weeks during their worklife.

It is difficult to provide a quantitative estimate of these effects, but, given the large costs imposed on retirement by a double tax scheme (see Table 2–1), it is likely that workers' reactions would be substantial. Whatever the response, clearly it would not represent the distribution of work and consumption over the lifetime desired by individuals. Instead, equilibrium would be determined in an important way by a tax policy that levied special high income taxes on earnings used to support postponed consumption during retirement.

National Savings

We can also ask whether distortions in retirement patterns caused by an alternative pension tax policy imply reductions in national savings. The alternative tax policy is defined as one that does not grant tax-exempt status to pension trust funds. To the extent that savings are negatively affected by an alternative tax policy, a second-round impact on capital accumulation occurs, resulting in reductions in overall wage levels in the long run.

It is not obvious whether savings for retirement increase or decrease under an alternative pension tax policy. To the extent that retirement behavior is unaffected by the new policy, the national savings rate would *increase*. Recall from the above example that to maintain the retirement age of 65 and a retirement consumption of $6.66 per year, the worker must save $3.33 per year without a pension, but only $2.43 per year with a pension. In other words, to accumulate the same amount to support consumption during retirement by age 65, a worker must have a higher rate of savings to offset the taxes assessed during the accumulation period.

On the other hand, because the cost of retirement increases, either the retirement age will be postponed or annual retirement consumption will be reduced, or both. These effects work to *decrease* the rate of retirement savings. In the above example, either if retirement age was postponed until 68 or annual consumption during retirement was reduced from $6.66 to $4.86 per year, the worker could maintain the savings rate he had with a tax-exempt pension.

It is not obvious which effect would dominate. Available estimates, however, suggest that pensions increase overall savings. Estimates suggest that for each $1 of pension savings, roughly 50 cents is saved in the absence of pensions.[26] In short, if pensions are replaced by ordinary savings vehicles, the savings rate for retirement consumption likely would be reduced by about half. This would imply a slower rate of capital accumulation, which, over the long run, would reduce overall wages levels in the United States.[27]

THREADS OF A NATIONAL RETIREMENT POLICY

The above discussion helps make it apparent that current tax policy towards pensions is not intended to promote long and prosperous retirement periods. Instead, it represents a policy of keeping the government neutral in workers' retirement decisions. Not awarding pension trust funds tax-exempt status is the equivalent of the government actively discouraging early retirement and consumption during retirement. The government influences decisions in this alternative world by imposing a special tax on earnings used to support consumption during older ages.

Other recent legislative activity by the Congress has been reenforcing the theme of letting individual choice determine retirement decisions. Two changes were made in 1977 and 1983 to eliminate important features in the social security system, which previously provided strong influences on individuals' retirement decisions.

Prior to 1977, the social security annuity formula was a function of *nominal* wage histories of retiring workers. The lowest five years of earnings were eliminated before average earnings were calculated. Solely because of increasing wages over time (due to economy-wide productivity increases and inflation), workers could substantially increase their social security annuities by continuing to work, thereby replacing inflation-eroded earnings in the early 1950s with current-dollar wages earned at older ages. This provided a strong incentive to continue working, perhaps as late as age 65, when the earnings test encouraged retirement (see below).[28]

In 1977, Congress changed the social security rules so that workers' earnings histories were adjusted by a national wage index up to levels that prevailed during the year the worker turned age 60. Thus, 1953 wages, for example, were restated in terms of current wage levels at age 60. This ruling eliminated most of the artificial incentive to keep working beyond optimal retirement ages determined in a free market, and instead let individual choice and productivity effects dominate the retirement decision.

While this change in policy reduced the social security system incentive to postpone early retirement, it left in place another provision—called the *earnings test*—which provided incentives for workers to retire no later than age 65. If an age-65 individual continued to work, he would lose 50 cents in social security benefits for each one dollar in wages earned. This was the equivalent of adding a 50 percent income tax on top of ordinary income taxes.[29]

While this individual could evade the explicit tax by postponing receipt of his social security benefits until he stopped work, he would not eliminate the effective tax imposed by the rule. If an age-65 worker continued to work for one more year, he would forgo one year's worth of social security benefits. In return, he would be awarded a slightly (3 percent) higher annuity beginning in the next year. However, since the present value of the higher annuity is substantially less than the benefits forgone during his age-65 work year, this option also acted like a special extra tax on work past age 65.[30] This tax rate was not trivial.[31]

In the Social Security Amendments Act of 1983, Congress did not eliminate the earnings test as such (though it reduced the rate from 50 to 33 percent), but it did act to gradually eliminate the penalty for work after age 65. In this way, one year's worth of forgone social security benefits are offset entirely by an increase in the annuity starting at a later retirement age. However, the penalty is to be removed gradually. The system is expected to be completely neutral on the decision whether to work after age 65 only by the year 2005.

While the impact of the 1983 law will not be fully effective for some time, it completes the policy begun in 1977 to substantially reduce government influences on the decision to retire. Once full equilibrium is attained, the social security system, following a long period of perhaps influencing the retirement decision in an important way, no longer will exert important artificial barriers to individuals' retirement decisions.[32] In addition, as noted above, the exemption of half of all social security benefits from taxation also is scheduled to be gradually eliminated over a lengthy period of time.

Once these changes are fully effective, social security policies will be consistent with a national pension tax policy that creates neutrality on the part of the federal government concerning individuals' decisions to retire. At the same time, the social security system addresses Congressional concern that all workers have "adequate" income during retirement. All workers—including "spenders" who might otherwise take advantage of "savers" when they attain old age—are required to contribute part of their earnings to a system designed to provide some minimum level of support during old age. In addition, the system is deliberately skewed to ensure that wage replacement rates are extraordinarily high for lower-wage workers.

It cannot be concluded, however, that this emerging federal policy implies that the government will leave the retirement decision entirely to the private sector. A fair reading of government actions in recent years implies a tendency to interfere with corporate retirement policies. Actions recently taken in this direction include the elimination of mandatory retirement policies and restrictions on the actuarial penalties imposed by most defined benefit pensions on older workers.[33]

For the most part, however, Congress continues to permit firms to influence the retirement decisions amongst their workers through a system of incentives to discourage "early" or "late" departure from the firm (see Chapter 1). This policy leaves the retirement decision to individuals and firms. As long as the government itself does not influence the retirement decision, older workers, even though encouraged to leave their main jobs at some point in their career, will not be discouraged from finding new jobs after taking their primary retirement.[34]

The next chapter builds on the essential threads of a national retirement policy that has government neutral in retirement decisions. The chapter begins the process of evaluating the tension between this policy, some of which is quite new, and other legislation, some of which is quite old, that interferes with savings and retirement decisions made in a free market. Evaluation of these policies in light of a more neutral national retirement policy may lead to a rethinking and revision of some perhaps outdated remnants of an older, more interventionist policy.

ENDNOTES

1. An exception occurs when the government attaches a tax on a market to correct an externality. For example, a pollution tax might align market incentives to account for effects on individuals not participating in the market.
2. That is, ($3.49 − $2.89)/$3.49 = 17.1%. In real terms, $3.49 is worth $1, and $2.89 is worth $.827.

3. See previous footnote.
4. That is, since the inflation rate is 5 percent in the example, then deflating $3.49 to age-40 dollars amounts to $1.
5. Roughly 44 percent of households headed by a 45 to 54-year-old (the most likely group of pension savers) have incomes in excess of $40,000, which likely makes them subject to the 28 percent marginal tax rate (taxable income for a joint income tax return must have taxable income equal to approximately $30,000 to face the 28 percent tax rate). Roughly 11 percent have incomes less than $10,000, likely making them exempt from taxation (owing to the standard deduction and personal exemptions). Since pension participants tend to have higher incomes, a 1:1 split between the 15 and 28 percent marginal rates seems reasonable.
6. Pension benefits in 1985 were $92 billion (Table 1–4). Assuming that these benefits have increased in nominal terms by 20 percent through 1989, puts the 1989 estimate at approximately $110 billion.
7. For an estimate of government pensions in relation to private sector amounts, see Ippolito, *Pensions, Economics, and Public Policy*, Chapter 5.
8. These estimates differ from the Joint Committee on Taxation numbers (see Chapter 1) because my estimates (a) exclude the effects of income smoothing (see next section in text) and (b) are based on a lifetime present value calculation. Congressional estimates are made on a cash accounting basis which offsets current contributions by current benefit payments. In a system that is growing, this method overstates the revenue impact of the pension tax provisions.
9. Some taxpayers, however, effectively face a marginal tax rate of 33 percent.
10. Households with less than $10,000 in income are likely to escape taxation owing to the standard deduction and personal exemption. Roughly 11 percent of households headed by 45 to 54-year-olds have incomes less then $10,000; 36 percent of over-age-65 households have incomes less than $10,000. This implies that 25 percent of households might shift from a 15 percent to a zero percent tax bracket when they retire.

    Married individuals filing joint returns must have gross family income in excess of $40,000 to be in the 28 percent tax bracket (in reality 33 percent—see footnote 9). Roughly 44 percent of households headed by a 45 to 54-year-old have income in excess of $40,000; only 14 percent of over-age-65 households have this level of income. These data suggest that 30 percent of households could shift from a 28 to a 15 percent tax rate during retirement. Data source: *Statistical Abstract of the U.S.*, 1988, p. 423.
11. This means that taxes owed on pensions would be calculated without consideration of deductions and exemptions.
12. Operationally, the calculation might work like income averaging prior to the Tax Reform Act of 1986. Upon retirement, individuals could be required to report the marginal tax rate over some sample of work years; this would be the rate against which all pension income would be taxed in the future.
13. This would be relatively easy in defined contribution plans since contributions are explicit. In defined benefit plans, this approach might well be intractable.
14. The reason is that revenue from taxation of social security benefits goes to the social security trust fund and is part of the equation that describes long-term solvency in the system.
15. See footnote 32 below.
16. See *Social Security Bulletin*, Annual Statistical Supplement, 1987, p. 102.
17. For example, male worker participation after age 65 in 1984 was only one half of

its value in 1940. See, U.S. Department of Commerce, Bureau of the Census, *Statistical Abstract of the United States*, 1984. Also, see Richard A. Ippolito, "Towards Explaining Earlier Retirement After 1970," *Industrial & Labor Relations Reviews* (1990), forthcoming.

18. For example, using the database from the U.S. Department of Labor's Survey of Pension Benefit Amounts, I found that only 4 percent of the retirees covered by pension plans retired after "normal" retirement age (usually age 65).
19. That is, one minus the tax rate (1 – .266), times the nominal interest rate (.075), less the inflation rate (.055), is zero.
20. The amount $3.33 times 30 years of work is $100.
21. That is, if $2.43 (real) is saved during each of 30 years and accumulates at a real interest rate of 2 percent, the amount $100 (real) will be available in year 30.
22. That is, $.90 is 13.5 percent of $6.66.
23. That is, the solution to $(45 - y) \times \$2.43 = y \times \$6.66$, where y is the number of retirement years, is $y = 12$.
24. The solution to $30 \times \$2.43 = 15X$, where X is retirement consumption, is $X = \$4.86$.
25. In a study I did of retirement for a cross section of workers that retired in the 1960s, I found that there was at least a one-to-one relationship between earlier retirement and more hours of work during work years. See Richard Ippolito, "Income Tax Policy and Lifetime Labor Supply," *Journal of Public Economics* (April 1985), pp. 327–347.
26. See Peter Diamond and Jerry Hauseman, "Individual Retirement and Savings Behavior," *Journal of Public Economics* (February 1984), pp. 81–114; Louis Dicks-Mireaux and Mervyn King, "Pension Wealth and Household Savings: Tests of Robustness," *Journal of Public Economics* (February 1984), pp. 115–140; and Alicia Munnell, "Private Pensions and Saving: New Evidence," *Journal of Political Economy* (October 1976), pp. 1013–1031. Also see Martin Feldstein, "Do Private Pensions Increase National Saving?" *Journal of Public Economics* (December 1978), pp. 277–293.
27. Two factors might ameliorate the personal savings effect. First, if the government used the new tax revenues to reduce existing debt, the increase in government savings might offset the reduction in personal savings. Second, in a world capital market, a lower U.S. savings rate would be spread across international labor markets, thereby softening the impact on U.S. wages alone.
28. See Alan Blinder et al., "Reconsidering the Work Disincentives of Social Security," *National Tax Journal* (December 1980), pp. 431–442.
29. In 1987, workers could earn up to $8,400 per year before the special earnings test was triggered. The threshold amount is indexed to the overall social security wage base.
30. See Richard Burkhauser and John Turner, "Can Twenty-Five Million Americans Be Wrong? A Response to Blinder, Gordon, and Wise," *National Tax Journal* (December 1981), pp. 467–472.
31. To illustrate, since wages are now indexed in the formula, then, with little consequence, I can ignore the recalculation effect that might occur because wages at age 65 might be higher than average real wages. An actuarially fair adjustment is roughly 8.3 percent per year. Thus, the amount of lost benefits for working the 65th year amount to roughly 5 percent (8.3 percent actuarially fair rate minus the 3 percent actually paid), times the number of retirement years left to death. If these years number 12, the tax would be 60 percent (5 percent penalty times

12 years), times annual benefits. If benefits replaced 60 percent of final wage (see Table 3–2 below), the tax rate on earnings equals 36 percent.

32. The social security system could have exerted important influences on retirement behavior even apart from the incentive effects discussed above because the system awarded important "wealth effects" (present value benefits greatly exceeded the present value of contributions). This action itself may have stimulated early retirement for many workers. But since these wealth effects have been diminishing gradually, these effects are expected to evaporate for workers retiring in the next century. See, for example, Robert Moffitt, "Trends in Social Security Wealth by Cohort," in *Economic Transfers in the United States*, edited by M. Moon (Chicago: University of Chicago Press, 1977), and Alicia Munnell, *The Future of Social Security* (Washington, D.C.: Brookings Institution, 1977). Also see Ippolito, "Towards Explaining."

    All of these studies were done before the 1983 amendments were enacted: retirement age with full benefits was increased gradually from 65 to 67; a new schedule of higher contribution rates was put into effect; and, as discussed in the text, half of all benefits will ultimately be subject to income taxation. These changes virtually ensure that the wealth effects for cohorts retiring after 2020 will be close to zero. See M.J. Boskin and D.J. Puffert, "The Financial Impact of Social Security by Cohort under Alternative Financing Assumptions," NBER Working Paper No. 2225, April 1987.

33. Actuarial penalties can still be imposed as shown in Chapter 1, but firms can no longer simply stop crediting service or freeze wages in the benefit formula solely because the worker reaches normal retirement age.

34. This essentially describes the system of retirement in Japan. See Kingsley Davis, "Retirement as a Dubious Paradise—Another Point of View," in *Issues in Contemporary Retirement*, edited by E. Lazear and R. Ricardo–Campbell (Stanford CA: Hoover Institution Press, 1988).

CHAPTER 3

Implementing a Neutral Pension Tax Policy

The last chapter showed that the federal government has been gravitating toward a national retirement policy that keeps the retirement decision in the domain of individual choice, subject to contracts freely entered into by workers and firms. Some of this policy is old. Pension tax policy dates back to 1926, though it had virtually no meaning until the income tax became an important institution in the United States during World War II (see Chapter 1). On the other hand, some income tax policy is quite new. Conforming the social security system to the same neutral policy was begun in 1977 and 1983 and will not be fully effective for two decades. If a neutral policy is to be pursued, we must ask which federal pension tax and related laws need to be reconsidered to complete the transition to a free-market system of retirement.

CONTRIBUTION LIMITS

I will start by reviewing current pension policies that already are consistent with a noninterventionist government role. First, existing tax policy extends to defined contribution plans. A more paternalistic policy might confine tax benefits to defined benefit pension plans in which firms presumably share investment risks. Second, the tax policy is applicable to plans that award lump-sum benefits. A more interventionist policy might award the tax rules only to plans that pay annuities until death and require joint and survivor annuities for spouses until their death.[1] Third, pensions are permitted to invest in a broad spectrum of portfolios that can include all bonds, all stock, and some holdings of "risky" securities like venture capital and small firm stocks. Pensions are not required to hold only "safe" securities like bonds or "blue chip" stocks.[2] Firms can offer, and individuals can choose, among plans that offer different kinds of risk and different streams of consumption during the retirement period.

Limits, however, are imposed on the amounts that can be contributed to pension trust funds. For example, in defined contribution plans, the limit is $30,000 in contributions per worker per year (or 25 percent of compensation, whichever is lower). The $30,000 contribution limit is indexed to prices, but starting only after inflation accumulates in the amount of 33 percent; thus, the limit in real terms in the long run is $22,500.[3]

Presumably, these limits are intended to restrict the consumption tax properties of pension trust accounts without, at the same time effectively converting the entire income tax system into a consumption tax scheme. For example, if there were no restrictions on defined contribution plans, wealthy individuals presumably could hold all their assets in these plans, taking advantage of their tax-exempt status. The next chapter discusses the issue of restricting the tax-exempt provision to retirement savings *only*—one that has provoked a reconsideration of tax policy towards pensions.

The Tax Reform Act of 1986, subject to a transitional rule, set an overall limit of $112,500 (indexed to prices beginning in 1988) as the maximum annuity from tax-deferred vehicles.[4] Withdrawals from defined contribution plans in the form of lump sums can occur up to five times this amount over any consecutive five-year period. Amounts beyond this are subject to a special excise tax of 15 percent, intended to offset at least a substantial portion of the tax advantages embedded in pension annuities (recall Table 1–2).

From an efficiency perspective, why the consumption tax principle should not be extended to other savings besides retirement savings is not clear. The same reasoning used to justify tax-exempt status for pension savings can be used to justify tax-exempt status for other savings accounts as well. Taxation of interest and dividends works in the general direction of discouraging any type of postponed consumption and therefore works to reduce aggregate savings.[5] If the consumption tax principle is extended to all savings vehicles, however, the issue arises concerning how the reduced federal tax revenue will be offset.

There is much literature dealing with the efficiency effects of a broad-based consumption tax and the problems of implementing such a system in place of an income tax.[6] It is neither appropriate nor necessary to introduce this discussion here, except to note that in a consumption tax system, pension trust funds are not treated differently from any other saving accumulation vehicle, and thus presumably play a smaller role in providing savings for retirement.[7]

In this volume, I will keep the discussion about pensions in the context of the existing income tax system and will limit the discussion to policy options that are either tax neutral or revenue increasing (for example, see proposals in Chapter 2). Thus, I simply accept the payout limit on overall tax-deferred income as a constraint on the system.

RESTRICTION OF TAX POLICY TO FIRM-OFFERED PENSIONS

The concern with limiting the tax-exempt status to pension trust funds is a natural outgrowth of applying consumption tax principles to vehicles designed to finance one subset of savings motives, namely, those aimed at supporting retirement consumption. As might be anticipated, this special tax status invites attempts to "overuse" these vehicles. Limits on payouts are ways to reduce "overuse" by higher-income workers. As we shall see in the next chapter, limits on contributions are designed to prevent stockholders from, in effect, using these funds as personal savings accounts of sorts. All of these problems would evaporate if Congress replaced the income tax with a consumption tax. Without such a change, regulatory costs designed to restrict the size of pension accounts are expected.

There are other regulatory and efficiency costs inherent in the current system, unrelated to enforcing limits on the system. These costs are attributable to the remnants of a system that had, and has, the government directly intervening with savings and retirement decisions that ought to be determined by individuals and firms. This body of regulation is the subject of this section.

The Preference Principle

The biggest shortcoming of pension tax policy in the United States is that tax-exempt status is not given to all savings vehicles for retirement. With inconsequential exceptions,[8] special tax status for pensions is reserved for firm-offered pension plans. For reference, we can call this the *preference principle* in current tax policy. In order for workers to take advantage of the national tax policy for pension savings, they must entrust their implicit pension savings to firms that, in turn, promise to return these monies at some later date.

Pension regulation. In essence, this peculiar application of pension tax policy creates potential *agency problems*. The law effectively forces workers to entrust their savings with a nonfinancial institution—partnerships and corporations mostly. Since these institutions are not otherwise covered by existing financial regulations, Congress has erected new machinery to regulate the potential agency problems that Congress, itself, created.

Most of these laws are embodied in the Employee Retirement Security Act of 1974 (ERISA) and related Internal Revenue Service Code rules. These laws include fiduciary regulations, reporting requirements, vesting rules, funding rules and restrictions on benefit formulas.

In addition, the laws include mandatory federal insurance for defined benefit pensions. When a plan sponsor fails with underfunded pensions and is unable to make up the difference, the Pension Benefit Guaranty Corporation assumes the pension obligation.

Ironically, while undoubtedly imposing large costs on pension plans, the regulations actually have not apparently resulted in fewer agency problems or even reduced the potential for fraud[9] perpetrated by firms intent on cheating workers. The evidence suggests that pension promises are generally honored, a fact that is attributable to reputation and other mechanisms that operate in the private market, not to government regulation.[10]

What the regulation has succeeded in doing, besides raising the costs of operating pension plans (especially defined benefit plans), is to create a mechanism (through the insurance company) to transfer billions of dollars from workers in well-funded, viable firms to those in unfunded plans in dying industries. Because the insurance is not based on market prices, the system encourages large unhealthy firms to sponsor generous, unfunded pension plans on the assumption that workers in other firms will pay for them. The moral hazards created by the insurance have led to even more regulation and more interference with the operation of the private pension system.[11]

Anti-discrimination rules. The argument for the preference principle in current tax policy is buried in the Internal Revenue Code antidiscrimination rules. These rules were enacted in the Revenue Act of 1942. With some exceptions, the rules require firms to cover most of their workers, regardless of pay level, under the same plan and to treat all participants in the plan alike.[12] Ostensibly, these rules are designed to limit higher-wage workers from "overusing" the pension plan; to increase pension savings rates for lower-income earners; and perhaps to engineer some cross subsidies from high- to low-wage earners outside the federal budget.

The antidiscrimination rules make it likely that heterogeneous groups of employees will be covered by the same pension plan, virtually ensuring that most workers will have nonoptimal savings rates. Workers who want to save for higher levels of retirement consumption cannot do so except outside the pension system. Since this approach is costly (see Chapters 1 and 2), most likely these workers will be induced to retire later and consume less during retirement than they would prefer. These distortions on individual choice impose efficiency costs like those discussed in Chapter 2 (see Figure 2–1).

At the same time, those who otherwise would prefer to save less and perhaps have later retirement or lower consumption during retirement or who have some other source of wage replacement besides pensions (like low-wage earners that receive disproportionate replacement rates from the social security system [see below]) are essentially forced to forgo more current consumption than they would prefer. Since these workers are forced to save more than they prefer, predictably, they will retire prematurely.

Supporters of the discrimination rules apparently either assume or are hopeful that one outcome of the rules is an off-budget transfer from high- to low-income workers. The numbers in Tables 1–2 and 2–1 demonstrate that the value of pension savings is greater for individuals subject to higher marginal income-tax rates. In effect, these individuals face greater effective income taxes if they save for retirement outside the pension system. Since lower-income workers may face low tax rates or pay no tax at all, they tend to be indifferent to saving in a pension plan or some outside vehicle.

The discrimination rules restrict the use of different plans for different workers in the firm on the basis of wage levels. This restriction suggests that higher-income workers might agree to "bribe" lower-income workers into accepting a more generous pension plan by paying them higher cash wages. These wage subsidies are financed by higher tax benefits available from a more generous plan to higher-wage workers. Put another way, the pension tax policy is a way to "rebate" the extra income tax assessed on earnings for future consumption inherent in the income tax system. The discrimination rules may effectively cause higher-wage earners to lose part of this rebate, thereby recreating the so-called second tax on future consumption except that the extra "tax" revenue goes directly to low-wage earners instead of passing through the Treasury. For their part, lower-wage workers receive hidden subsidies in the form of higher pension benefits, which work in the direction of encouraging them to leave the work force at earlier ages.

In addition, the antidiscrimination rules essentially require the firm to impose the same quit costs and the same incentives to retire on all workers in the firm, regardless of wage levels. This constraint can be costly if it is important for the firm to provide special incentives to some of its workers, say the higher-paid employees. If the firm were free to stylize pensions for different segments of the work force, it could set up different generosity parameters and accrual rates, thus imposing different magnitudes of costs on those who quit "too early" or stay "too late."

Those workers in the firm for which these behavioral patterns pose smaller productivity effects might, for example, be offered a smaller defined benefit plan or one with different rules or a defined contribution plan that would give them the opportunity to leave the firm at the time they chose, without forgoing part of their pension benefits. Constraining the firm's ability to offer more diverse pensions across its work force, ensures that the firm will impose penalties that are too low for some workers and too high for others. Thus, overall firm productiv-

FIGURE 3–1 Pension Coverage at Age 50

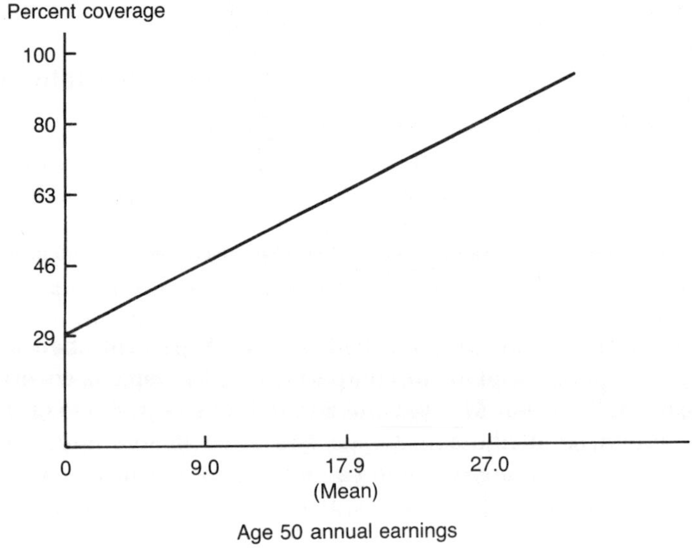

SOURCE: Stuart Dorsey, "A Model and Empirical Estimates of Worker Pension Coverage in the U.S.," *Southern Economic Journal* 49 (October 1982), 506–20.

dition, the wage replacement ratio has been deliberately skewed to provide transfers from high- to low-income workers.

Social security wage replacement rates are shown in Table 3–2. The data apply to 1976 but are not qualitatively different from current replacement rates.[17] Workers earning about 40 percent of the median wage ("low" wage in the table) receive wage replacement rates roughly double those earning incomes equal to the maximum taxable wage base. Males 65-year-old with low earnings and with spouses also age 65 have replacement rates equal to almost 100 percent. If these workers are also covered by a pension, they have combined replacement rates far in excess of 100 percent.[18]

Not surprisingly, these replacement rates generate unusually early retirement amongst low-wage earners. Table 3–3 provides estimates of the probability of accepting social security benefits at the earliest permissible age (62) for a sample of workers eligible to receive benefits in 1973. The earnings threshold in 1973, at which the earnings test was applied, was $2,100. Thus, some portion of those earning $2,100 might

TABLE 3–2 Social Security Replacement Rates

Type of Beneficiary	*Earnings*		
	Low	*Median*	*Maximum†*
Male, Age 65			
Single	66.3	46.2	33.0
With wife‡	99.4	69.3	49.5
Male, Age 62			
Single	53.0	36.9	26.4
With wife‡	77.9	54.3	38.7

†Low, median, and maximum wages in 1975 were $3,439, $8,255 and $14,100.
‡Same age as spouse.

NOTE: Numbers in table are percents.

SOURCE: Alicia Munnell, *The Future of Social Security* (Washington, D.C.: Brookings Institution, 1977), p. 26.

have accepted social security at age 62 and continued to work. For other wage levels, social security acceptance likely implies retirement from the work force. The numbers hold constant other factors that might also affect the retirement decision, including private pension coverage, education, and marital status.

The results show that workers earning roughly one third of median earnings, or $2,100 per year, had a 56.5 percent early acceptance rate. As stated above, since the earnings test exempts all $2,100 in earnings from the earnings test, some of these recipients might have remained in the work force and still collected their social security benefits. Those with earnings equal to two thirds of the median wage had a 37.5 percent acceptance rate, while those with wages 50 percent higher than the median wage had only a 5.7 percent early acceptance rate. It is not surprising that a system that provides such high wage replacement benefits to low-wage earners encourages their relatively early exit from the workforce. The numbers question the need—and dramatically suggest the likely effect of—imposing subsidized private pensions on top of the social security system for low-wage earners.

Integration rules. In fact, until 1986, federal tax policy incorporated this kind of reasoning. By permitting private plans to *integrate* their benefits with the social security system, firms could offset private pension payments in consideration of social security benefits received by workers. This policy had the effect of permitting firms to escape some of the impact of discrimination rules because firms could at least account for different savings preferences and different incentive effects as they varied from high- to low-income workers.

Unfortunately, in the Tax Reform Act of 1986, the integration rules

TABLE 3–3 Age-62 Acceptance Rates under Social Security

Annual Earnings	*Percent*
$2,100	56.5
4,200	37.5
6,300 (mean)	21.2
8,400	10.0
9,700	5.7

NOTE: Estimates hold constant other factors that might affect age of acceptance, including private pension coverage, marital status, education, and total credits accumulated under the social security system. For workers with annual earnings less than $2,100, social security acceptance does not necessarily imply retirement because the earnings test did not apply to this level of earnings at the time of the study.

SOURCE: Richard Burkhauser, "The Early Acceptance of Social Security," *Industrial Labor Relations Review* 33 (1980), pp. 484–492.

were altered substantially. Integration can still be a feature of private pension plans, but the degree to which high- and low-income workers can be affected by the rules is substantially diminished.[19]

PROPOSAL FOR A MORE EFFICIENT PENSION TAX POLICY

In essence, the exclusion of tax policy toward firm-offered pensions and related discrimination rules conflict with other legislation enacted to reduce the influence of the government on private retirement decisions. The neutrality principles inherent in the tax-exempt status of pension trust funds and the new social security policies to eliminate incentive effects for the system are contradicted by the preference for firm-offered pensions and consequent discrimination rules.

Tax policy towards retirement savings can be made more consistent with a national policy that has a more neutral influence on retirement age if two simple but important changes are made in the Internal Revenue Code: *First, the limit on contributions to individual retirement accounts should be increased to the levels applicable to defined contribution plans; and second, tax rules covering IRAs should be made identical to those covering firm-offered pension plans.* These changes are the equivalent of repealing the preference principle in current tax policy towards pensions. The payout limit on tax-deferred income ($112,500 indexed to prices beginning in 1988) can be retained because it already accommodates payouts from IRAs.

These simple changes would create a competition between IRAs and firm-offered pension plans. If firm-offered plans resulted in either sufficiently higher firm productivity (and thus higher wages) or sufficiently high group annuity benefits, presumably they would survive. Otherwise, all savings for retirement would be made through IRAs.

To permit firm-offered pensions to compete fairly with individual retirement accounts, most regulatory constraints on firm-offered pension plans should be eliminated. The repeal of the preference principle from pension tax policy essentially would eliminate the agency problem. Firms that presumably are marginal candidates for sequestering workers' retirement savings would not survive as sponsors of pension plans.[20] Presumably, only firms with strong reputations would survive the market test. In any event, since the federal government would offer workers the choice whether to use firm-offered pensions or IRAs (or some combination, subject to the overall payout limit during retirement), there would be less argument for federal regulation of agents that survived the new policy.

However, some regulations, such as fiduciary rules aimed at preventing misappropriation of funds and the like, should be continued. These regulations are parallel to those that cover commercial and investment banks, mutual funds, and insurance companies, presumably the institutions that will and do offer individual retirement accounts. Other regulatory apparatus, however, should be dismantled, including vesting rules, discrimination rules, social security integration rules, minimum funding rules, mandatory insurance, benefit accrual rules, contribution limits (which are redundant to the payout limit on total tax-deferred income[21]), and other nuisance constraints on incentives permitted in private pension plans.[22]

With firms free to set their own pension rules, unencumbered by regulatory constraints, pensions could be designed to generate the optimal combination of productivity effects and individual choice. If workers chose these plans either to fully or partially replace their IRA options, then we could conclude that surviving firm-offered pension plans would be characterized by substantial productivity or group annuity benefits.

Individuals would be free to supplement these plans (subject to the payout limit) or to subscribe exclusively to one or many IRA combinations and to work for firms that offered no pension benefits. These IRAs could include annuity contracts from insurance companies or various types of lump-sum accounts characterized by various levels of risk. If pooling effects are important, the firm could act as a collection agent of sorts to give workers access to group contracts available from institutions (like insurance companies) offering IRAs.

Tax rules for IRAs. As a final matter, to be competitive, IRAs must enjoy the same tax status as firm-offered pensions. This means that all contributions must be tax deductible, and IRA trust funds must be tax exempt. All distributions should be treated as ordinary taxable income,

FIGURE 3–2 Tax Rates on Age 65 Consumption

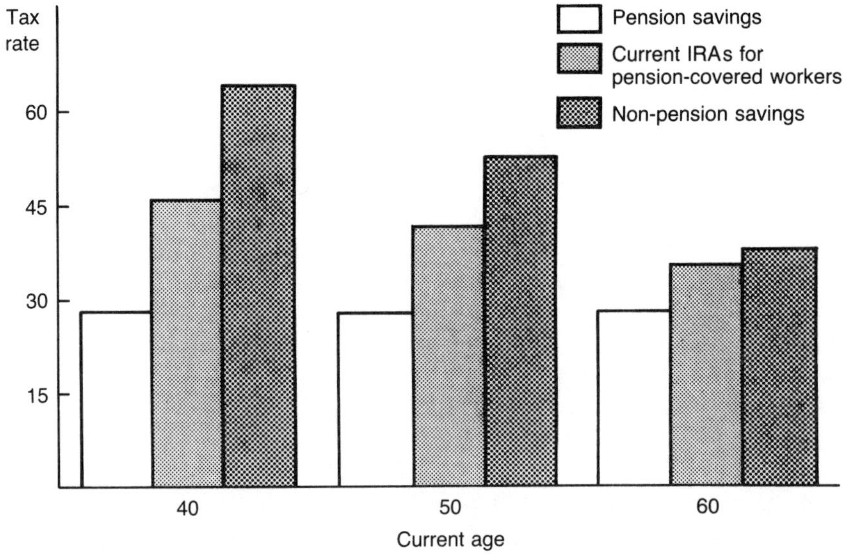

NOTES: Marginal tax rate: 28%. Interest rate: 10%.

perhaps segregated with other tax-deferred income to eliminate the income-smoothing effect now embedded in pension tax policy (see Chapter 2).

Current tax policy toward IRAs conforms to these rules, but only for workers not covered by firm-offered pensions.[23] IRAs held by pension-covered workers are taxed at higher rates than firm-offered pensions because they are taxed twice: First, earnings contributed to IRAs are subject to income tax. Second, when the earnings are withdrawn, all interest earned during the accumulation period is treated as ordinary income. Since interest earnings essentially represent the amount needed to adjust the value of earnings across periods, the tax on interest amounts to a second tax on the same earnings. Thus, the total tax is substantial in relation to the single tax levied against firm-offered pension plans. However, since the tax on interest earnings is deferred until retirement, the tax levy still is lower than the tax on ordinary tax-exposed savings accounts.

Figure 3–2 demonstrates (1) firm-offered pension tax policy, (2) current IRA tax policy for workers covered by pension plans, and (3) tax policy towards outside savings vehicles. The figures apply to an individual who pays a 28 percent tax rate on income; the interest rate is set at 10 percent. For age-40 workers, the effective tax rate applied against age-65 consumption for savings made through a pension plan is 28 percent. The tax rate on the same savings outside the pension plan is 64 percent. The tax rate for IRA accounts for workers already covered by a pension is between these numbers, or 46 percent. While better than a tax-exposed account, current IRA tax policy clearly is inferior to pension tax policy.

This discrepancy is easy to eliminate. Assuming that the smoothing effect is eliminated for private pension plans, a policy equivalent to pensions can be applied to IRAs. The policy can be effected either by subjecting contributions to IRAs to the normal income tax and treating distributions as tax-free income or by permitting deductions for IRA contributions from current taxation, but treating distributions from IRAs as taxable income during retirement. If the smoothing effect is not eliminated, the latter choice must be used to generate tax neutrality between IRAs and pension plans.[24]

CONCLUSION

The hallmark of pension tax policy is its preference for firm-offered pensions. This preference appears to have its roots in antidiscrimination rules embodied in the Revenue Act of 1942. The preference of tax policy for plans operated by firms (and other nonprofit organizations), as opposed to pension programs offered by financial organizations like banks and insurance companies, give rise to potential agency problems. These problems, in turn, are used to justify regulatory machinery to protect workers from being cheated by plan sponsors that might not be chosen as agents to invest retirement savings in the absence of the tax preference for firm-sponsored pension plans. The rules and the regulations they entail impose large and unnecessary costs on the U.S. economy.

The discrimination rules appear to be designed to limit the use of tax-exempt pension trust funds by high-wage earners, to force lower-wage workers to save more for their retirement, and to effect off-budget transfers from high- to low-wage earners. When the rules were enacted in 1942, they might have been the most effective means for accomplishing these goals. Almost 50 years later, however, these rules clearly are outdated.

The use of cheap, high-speed data processing now enables the Internal Revenue Service to monitor individual tax returns and thus to enforce payout limits on total tax-deferred income during retirement. Moreover, the social security system, which was in its infancy in 1942, now enjoys almost universal coverage, awards much higher benefits in real terms, and is specifically designed to generate extraordinary wage replacement rates for low-wage earners. Low-wage men retiring at age 65 have replacement rates from 66⅔ percent to 100 percent depending on their marital status and age of spouse. The system explicitly effects transfers from higher- to lower-wage earners. In short, intended transfers that might have attended the creation of the 1942 discrimination rules have been superceded by a more equitable, universal social security system.

In light of the changed conditions that now characterize the U.S. economy and its social programs, Congress should rethink the cost and effectiveness of a policy that almost surely is outmoded. This reassessment is particularly important now that the social security system has been restructured to substantially reduce its influence on retirement decisions. Allowing for a phase-in period, the social security system now reflects the same neutrality principles similar to those embedded in fundamental tax policy towards pension.

An effective way to expand the principle of neutrality in all aspects of tax policy towards retirement savings is to eliminate limits for contributions to individual retirement accounts (the payout limits for deferred earnings during retirement would be retained) and to make these accounts available to all workers on the same tax basis as firm-offered pension plans. These changes would effectively eliminate the potential agency problem created by the tax preference for firm-offered pensions and would create a competition between pension plans and the financial organizations that offer IRAs for workers' retirement savings. The overall payout limit for retirees of $112,500 (indexed), imposing a limit on the use of all pension and IRA plans for each worker, should be retained.[25]

With a fully competing IRA alternative in place, firms should be set free of most pension regulation, permitting them to arrange their plans in ways most likely to maximize worker benefits and labor productivity. The deregulation of pensions would require the repeal of most of the Employee Retirement Income Security Act and some parts of the Internal Revenue Code, notably discrimination rules, integration rules, and contribution limits. With these steps, the government would complete the building of a policy that leaves retirement decisions primarily in the domain of a free market.

ENDNOTES

1. Current law provides that all defined benefit plans offer joint and survivor annuities as their standard form of benefit payment, but workers may opt out of the provision if the worker and his/her spouse agree.
2. There are some restrictions that apply to most pension plans. Usually, a plan is not permitted to invest more than 10 percent of its holdings in the plan sponsor's own securities, and diversification across many securities is, in effect, required. "Prudence" is defined in terms of the risk and return of the entire portfolio, not particular investments.
3. Technically, the limit is tied to another limit in the tax code that puts a ceiling on projected benefit levels in defined benefit plans at $90,000, which was in-

dexed to the price level beginning in 1988. When this limit reaches $120,000, the $30,000 contribution limit is scheduled to be indexed to prices.

4. The maximum was set as the greater of $150,000 in nominal terms or $112,500 indexed to prices beginning in 1988. Thus, over some indeterminant period, the maximum permissible limit in real terms will be higher than depicted by $112,500 indexed to prices.
5. It has been estimated that if the income tax were replaced by a consumption tax in the United States, national income would increase by roughly one percent which, in present value terms, would be valued at more than one trillion dollars (1989 dollars). See Don Fullerton et al., "Replacing the Income Tax with a Progressive Consumption Tax," *Journal of Public Economics* 20 (1983), 3–23.
6. A small selection of this literature includes Henry Aaron, Harvey Galper, and Joseph Pechman, eds., *Uneasy Compromise: Problems of a Hybrid Income-Consumption Tax* (Washington, D.C.: Brookings Institution, 1988); Alan Auerbach and Martin Feldstein, *Handbook of Public Finance* (Amsterdam: North Holland Press, 1985); David Bradford, *Blueprints for Basic Tax Reform* (Washington, D.C.: U.S. Department of the Treasury, 1977); Nicholas Kaldor, *An Expenditure Tax* (London: Allen and Unwin, 1955); Robert Hall and Alvin Rabushka, *The Flat Tax* (Stanford: Hoover Institution, 1985); John Makin, *Real Tax Reform: Replacing the Income Tax* (Washington, D.C.: American Enterprise Institute, 1985); Joseph Pechman, *Federal Tax Policy*, 5th ed. (Washington, D.C.: Brookings Institution, 1987); and Charles Walker and Mark Bloomfield, *The Consumption Tax: A Better Alternative?* (Cambridge: Ballinger, 1987).
7. Pensions would still exist in such a world if they offered important advantages to workers and firms, including their potential effects on productivity and cost of annuities.
8. Individual Retirement Accounts (which limit contributions to $2,000 per year) and so-called Keough plans for self-employed individuals (which limit contributions to $7,000 per year) are also permitted under current law.
9. Here, fraud refers to cheating workers out of their expected pension benefits by firing them at older ages or terminating the pension plan.
10. See Richard A. Ippolito, "A Study of the Regulatory Effect of the Employee Retirement Security Act," *Journal of Law and Economics* (April 1988), 85–125; and Christopher Cornwell et al., "Opportunistic Behavior."
11. The most recent reforms are contained in the Pension Protection Act of 1987. For a complete discussion of the operation of the insurance, see Richard A. Ippolito, *The Economics of Pension Insurance* (Homewood, IL: Richard D. Irwin for the Pension Research Council, 1989).
12. Usually, it is permissible to have separate plans for blue- and white-collar workers, particularly if one or both plans cover unionized workers. If a firm has several subsidiaries, it need not cover all with the same plan.
13. Fiduciary and reporting rules are enforced by the U.S. Department of Labor; discrimination, funding, and vesting rules are enforced by the Internal Revenue Service; and the insurance program is operated by the Pension Benefit Guaranty Corporation.
14. These include the cost of completing government annual reports and other disclosure costs; special actuarial calculations; and consultants to ensure that the plans continue to conform to ever-changing federal regulations and legislation.
15. Recall that the limit is subject to a transitional rule as specified in note 4.
16. For example, it is well known that contribution limits in defined benefit plans are more likely constraining for younger workers compared to defined contribu-

tion plans. See E. Allen, et al., *Pension Planning*. In addition, they tend to discriminate against workers saving disproportionately late in their worklife for retirement.

17. For example, see the Social Security Administration, *Social Security Bulletin, Annual Statistical Supplement*, 1987.
18. The average primary pension plan has a replacement rate of 25 percent; roughly half of all plans have replacement rates higher than this.
19. The ways the new rules work are complex. But in a defined contribution plan, for example, if the highest-income participant ends up with a contribution rate to his account equal to 10 percent of salary then, after accounting for the integration formula, the lowest-income worker cannot receive less than a 5 percent contribution rate. See E. Allen et al., *Pension Planning*.
20. It might be possible, however, for these firms to act as collection agents of sorts to enable workers to obtain pooling advantages of IRAs from large financial institutions such as insurance companies.
21. See note 4.
22. These include, for example, rules that limit firms' ability to impose retirement incentives at normal retirement age and those that limit "backloading" of contributions towards later in the career with the firm.
23. Some exceptions are made for pension-covered workers who have an adjusted gross income below some threshold amount and for nonworking spouses.
24. In the absence of a smoothing effect, the present value revenue implications to the U.S. Treasury would be the same under either scheme. But the short-term flows would be quite different. If contributions are taxed, short-term revenues would increase dramatically.
25. See note 4.

CHAPTER 4

Controlling Pension Plan Overfunding

Since consumption tax principles have been extended to savings for retirement through pension plans, but not to other savings vehicles, it is predictable that taxpayers will try to "overuse" the pension vehicle. As discussed in Chapter 3, payout limits during retirement, established in the Tax Reform Act of 1986, limit the "overuse" of pensions by high-income workers. These limits do not, however, address the problem of stockholders overfunding their defined benefit plans: that is, retaining trust benefits in excess of amounts required to fund promised benefits.

In defined contribution plans, there is little opportunity to "overuse" the tax policy granted pensions. After short vesting periods, contributions made to these plans belong to workers. Thus, it is difficult for stockholders to use these accounts for purposes other than paying pensions. In defined benefit plans, however, though they theoretically follow the same funding logic as defined contribution plans (see Chapter 1), the one-to-one relationship between contributions (and workers' forgone wages) and benefits is lost. This separation creates the opportunity for stockholders to use the pension plan, in part, as a corporate savings account.

The extension of the tax-exempt principle to all savings accounts could be justified on the same efficiency grounds as pension tax policy. It would eliminate bias in the tax code against all savings, not just against savings for retirement. For the sake of avoiding the problems raised by the loss of tax revenue and to keep the discussion on pensions, I will avoid this issue. I accept as a constraint, that Congress, for whatever reason, has decided not to extend the consumption tax principle to nonretirement savings vehicles. If Congress cannot control the tax revenue implications of this policy directly, it will do so indirectly by distorting the operation of private pension plans or conceivably by

FIGURE 4–1 Funding Levels, 1978–1986

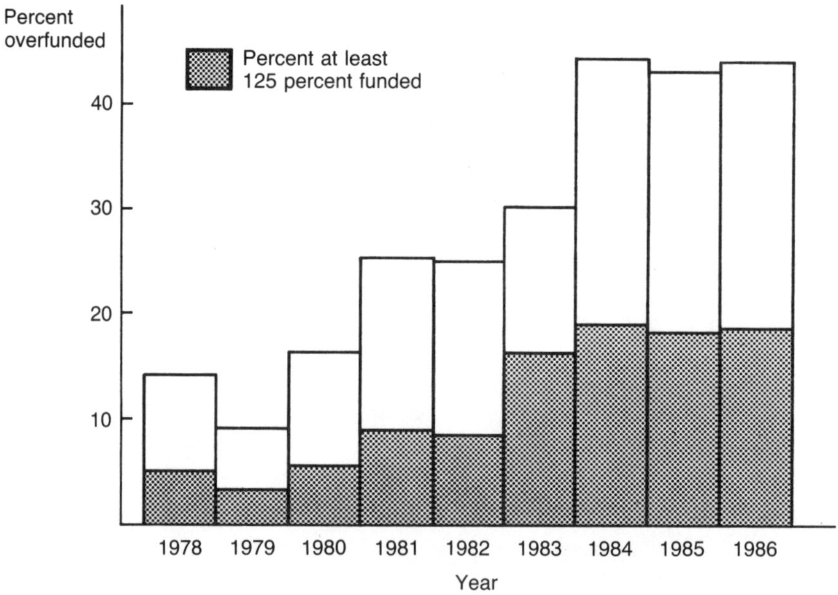

NOTES: Plans weighted by participants. Liabilities calculated using a 2% interest rate.
SOURCE: *Form 5500 Annual Pension Plan Reports*

limiting tax-exempt status to defined contribution plan trusts. Thus, the problem becomes one of effectively restricting the pension plan trust fund as a vehicle to accumulate only implicit worker savings for pensions at retirement and to effect the restrictions without imposing undue cost on plan sponsors.

The data in Figure 4–1 make it apparent that overfunding is routine in a large proportion of defined benefit plans. The figure shows the proportion of these plans (weighted by participants) that are overfunded in an ongoing sense during the period 1978–1986.[1] The funding ratios are understated in relation to maximum funding rules as set out in the Internal Revenue Code because my calculation of liabilities permits recognition of ad hoc inflation adjustments during retirement.[2] Technically, prefunding these increases is not permitted by the Internal Revenue Code (unless the adjustments are guaranteed as a part of the pension benefit). The figure shows that even during the late 1970s, following the large reductions in stock market values from 1972 to 1974,[3] approximately one in six plans was overfunded. In 1981, one in four plans was overfunded, and from 1984 to 1986, almost one in two.

TABLE 4–1 Overfunding in Relation to Ongoing Benefits, 1984

Funding Ratio	*Plans*	*Participants*
100–124	22.3	20.9
125–149	17.3	23.4
150 or more	22.1	17.6
Total	61.7	61.9

NOTE: Numbers in the table are percents. Liabilities do not reflect future ad hoc inflation adjustments during retirement. See note 4 in text.

SOURCE: Form 5500, *Annual Pension Plan Reports*; excludes plans with fewer than 100 participants.

To give an idea of the amount of understatement in these results, I recalculated the funding distribution for 1984 using liabilities that did not reflect anticipated ad hoc inflation adjustments for retirees. This calculation follows more closely the rules actually set out in the Code for permissible funding.[4] The results are shown in Table 4–1. Approximately three out of five plans (weighted by participants) were overfunded in terms of supposedly maximum funding limits intended by the code; one in four was at least 50 percent overfunded. Total overfunding amounted to $103 billion or over 16 percent of all assets held by defined benefit pension plans.[5]

This funding equilibrium was upset in 1987 when the Congress enacted new funding rules. Although the rules apparently were intended merely to reduce overfunding problems and thus control the tax revenue implications of pension tax policy,[6] I will show below that they are unlikely to be fully successful in accomplishing this purpose. Instead, the rules create a hidden tax on defined benefit plans and on low-risk pension portfolios. An alternative funding policy is developed that arguably is more successful in controlling overfunding and yet is free of distortion on the firm's choice of plan type and portfolio.

TAX BIAS AGAINST DEFINED BENEFIT PLANS

Impact of the New Funding Rules

As a way of illustrating the problems that have developed from the new rules, I will start by considering a firm that has no intentions of overusing the pension plan for the benefit of stockholders. The firm wishes to create a defined benefit plan and to invest funds exclusively in essentially risk-free Treasury bills. To illustrate the essence of the problem, I will start by reconsidering the same simple plan discussed in Chapter 1.

In this pension, the firm has one participant who just started work at age 40. Retirement age is 65, and the annual wage in real terms is

$10. Expected wage growth and the long-term nominal interest rate are 10 percent. To facilitate discussion in terms of real dollars, I will assume that the inflation rate is also 10 percent, which assumes that the real interest rate and real wage growth rates are zero. The terminology would change somewhat, but the results would be the same if the inflation rate were assumed to be, say 8 percent, and real wage growth and the real interest rate were each 2 percent. Also, recall that under the funding rules that prevailed prior to 1987, the firm could fund in proportion to the ongoing liabilities it accrued each year.

Since the pension in the example paid a lump sum equal to 10 percent, times years of service, times final wage, then in real terms, a total of $25 (10%, times 25 years of service, times final *real* wage $10) needed to be funded over the worker's 25 years with the firm, or $1 per annum in real terms. In actuarial terminology, an ongoing liability in the amount of one dollar is accrued each year. Prior to 1987, this was the permissible "normal" contribution to the plan.[7] This funding scenario is depicted in Figure 4–2 by the linear schedule beginning at zero and ending at $25 at the end of 25 years.

In 1987, Congress enacted the Omnibus Budget Reconciliation Act (OBRA), which imposed new maximum funding rules on defined benefit plans. Under the old rules, the firm was permitted to hold assets equal to *ongoing* benefits.[8] The new law constrains pension assets to be no more than 150 percent of *termination* benefits.[9] Termination benefits are different from ongoing benefits because termination benefits assume that the plan will be terminated immediately, while ongoing liabilities assume that the firm will continue and thus pay benefits in proportion to wage levels at retirement. When plans terminate, the pension obligation is determined using *existing* wages in the benefit formula. These benefits are frozen in nominal terms even though they are payable many years in the future at retirement age. Thus, unlike ongoing liabilities, termination benefits do not recognize that pension benefits are tied to wage at retirement, but instead assume that benefits are proportional to current wages.

The difference in calculations can be dramatic because inflation alone is expected to create a large wedge between current wages and wages at retirement.[10] To partly make up for the difference, the new tax rules permit firms to fund up to 150 percent of termination liabilities (but not more than 100 percent of ongoing liabilities). From the perspective of controlling funding, the new rules have appeal because, though the above simple example does not bring this out, ongoing liabilities involve numerous assumptions, permitting actuaries the opportunity to generate overfunding through use of assumptions that may not accurately portray the pension plan's circumstances.[11] In the termination calculation, the only assumption, besides mortality, is the interest

FIGURE 4–2 Trust Funding: Old and New Funding Rules

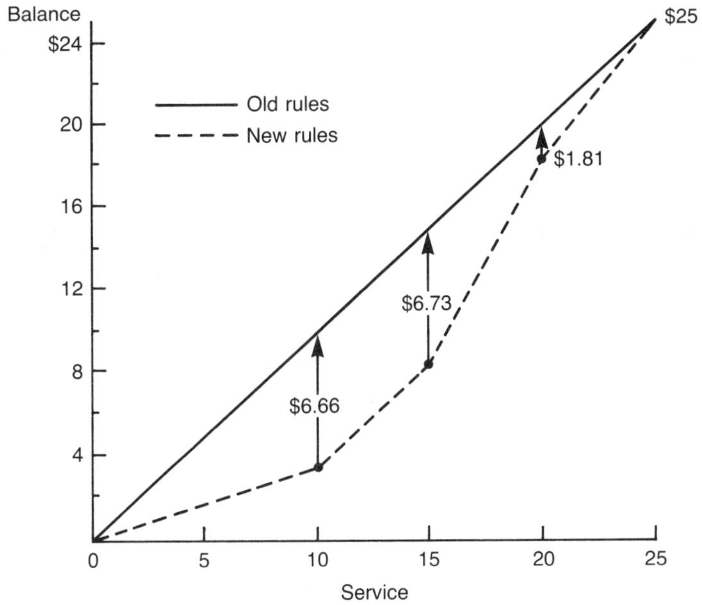

rate used to discount liabilities; and OBRA requires that this rate be determined by the U.S. Treasury.[12] In this section, I will discuss the tax bias introduced by the new rules.

The problem with the rules is that 150 percent of termination liabilities is often less than ongoing liabilities. The easiest way to illustrate this point is to calculate the value of termination benefits (PVT) for the 40-year-old worker in the example. In Chapter 1, it was shown that in year one ongoing liabilities equaled $1, and permissible contributions also were $1. However, 150 percent of termination benefits in year one is not $1, but only 12.3 cents.[13] Termination benefits are lower than ongoing benefits because termination benefits calculations do not project wages and thus discount benefits based on current wages, payable in the future. For a 40-year-old worker, one dollar in *nominal* terms payable in 25 years has a present value of only eight cents. An eight cent contribution will generate one dollar in *nominal* benefits in 25 years, not one dollar in *real* terms.

In contrast, the ongoing benefit reflects a 10 percent wage growth factor which offsets the 10 percent discount term. In other words, the ongoing calculation shows that a one-dollar contribution is required to

TABLE 4–2 Tax Cost of New Funding Rules

	Years of Service				
Category	*0*	*10*	*15*	*20*	*25*
Trust Balance ($real)					
1. Old rules	$0.00	10.00	15.00	20.00	25.00
2. New rules	0.00	3.34	8.27	18.19	25.00
3. Difference	0.00	6.66	6.73	1.81	0.00
4. Avg. diff. during interval	—	3.33	6.69	4.27	.90
Taxable Interest					
5. Avg. per year during interval	—	.33	.67	.42	.09
Tax During Interval					
6. 33% per year	—	.11	.22	.14	.03
7. Total for interval	—	1.10	1.10	.70	.15
8. Cumulative tax	—	1.10	2.20	2.90	3.05

NOTE: See text for assumptions.

pay for a *real* one-dollar benefit payable in 25 years. This is why, even allowing for multiplication by 150 percent, the termination funding limit is only approximately 12 percent of the ongoing liability limit in year one.

Recall from Chapter 1 that economic reality requires that workers pay for their pensions through forgone wages. Moreover, as long as workers commit themselves to the firm over the long run (which is presumably what the firm wants them to do), they will expect to receive real benefits at retirement, not termination benefits midstream. As such, competitive equilibrium requires—and the empirical evidence confirms—that workers will forgo wages in amounts sufficient to pay for ongoing benefits.[14] But, under the new funding rules, the firm can contribute only 12 percent of the worker's implicit one dollar contribution to the pension (in the form of forgone wages). Implicitly, 88 percent must be saved outside the trust. If the firm pays a tax rate of 33 percent, 88 percent of the implicit contribution accumulates at the after-tax 6.67 percent interest rate (10 percent, minus the 33 percent tax, times 10 percent).

Similar calculations apply to subsequent years. For example, in year 15 the trust fund is restricted to hold $8.27 in real terms.[15] Under the old funding rules, the pension trust could hold $15 in real terms in year 15. Thus, at the 15-year service level, the firm is accumulating $8.27 inside the pension trust at the before-tax interest rate and $6.73 outside the pension fund at the after-tax interest rate ($15 in real contributions minus $8.27 in the trust fund).

The maximum amount of assets in the trust fund under the new rules is shown by the nonlinear schedule in Figure 4–2 and the second row of Table 4–2. Row one in the table depicts the permissible amount in the trust when the firm was able to fund for ongoing benefits. The difference between the two rows in the table and the two schedules in the figure is the amount of accumulated savings that must be held outside the pension fund (row three of the table, also depicted in the figure).

Tax Assessment

It is easy to obtain an estimate of the tax impact of the new rules. Over each segment of the schedule in the figure, the average difference between the two trust accounts is calculated (row four in the table). Taxable interest is 10 percent times these differences (row five). The tax rate on these interest amounts is assumed to be 33 percent. Annual tax assessments on interest earned outside the trust are shown in row six.

Row seven lists the total tax assessment during each interval; for example, during the first 10 years, 11 cents in taxes are paid each year, amounting to $1.10 over 10 years. The last row accumulates these amounts. These numbers show that over 25 years an additional tax is paid on savings outside the pension under the new rules, amounting to approximately $3 in real terms, or 12 percent of the value of the pension, $25.

If, instead, the firm offers a defined contribution plan, it is entitled to deposit the full amount of the implicit pension contributions (forgone wages) into the pension trust fund, all of which accumulates at the pretax rate of interest. Because of OBRA's differential treatment of defined benefit and defined contribution plans, *a tax bias is created by the new full funding limits in favor of defined contributions plans.* Given the potential advantages of defined benefit plans to workers and firms (see discussion in Chapter 1), this tax distortion is expected to impose economic costs on workers and firms.

More General Results

Balanced work force. The use of a one-worker plan mimics the impact of the new law on new, growing firms with predominantly young workers, but it overstates the impact of the new rule in more mature firms. For older workers, 150 percent of termination liabilities can exceed ongoing liabilities. Since the rules are applied in the aggregate, the "surplus" amounts for older workers can be applied to the "deficit" amounts for younger workers. The new permissible trust balance is thus higher than depicted above for firms with a mix of younger and older workers. The tax effect, however, still is significant.

To illustrate, suppose in our sample firm that many workers, instead of one, are employed. Each worker starts at age 40 and retires at age 65. Workers never quit and are never fired. The firm is neither growing nor contracting; thus, employment is constant. For simplicity, assume that there are 25 workers in the firm. One worker joins each year, and one retires each year. These assumptions generate a work force comprised of one worker at each service level from one to 25.

Liabilities for the plan are obtained by adding the liability for each of 25 workers in the firm, each with a service level varying from zero to 25 years. Using the same assumptions as above, ongoing liabilities amount to $312.[16]

The termination value of benefits multiplied by 150 percent turns out to be $237,[17] or $75 less than ongoing liabilities. Thus, in the more general model, using a 10 percent interest rate, the new 150 percent full funding limit permits 75 percent ($237/$312) of ongoing liabilities to be funded; the remaining 25 percent must be saved in a tax-exposed vehicle. Thus, interest earnings on the $75 are subject to the corporate tax.

If the tax rate is 33 percent, and interest earnings are $7.50 (10 percent interest rate times $75), the effective tax levied against pension savings is $2.50 per year (33% tax times $7.50 in interest earnings). This tax amounts to approximately 10 percent of annual benefit payouts (recall that in the example, one retiree per year receives a $25 lump-sum payout).

Workers and retirees. Finally, I recalculated the tax for a plan that had three participants retired and receiving annuities for every 10 active workers. This example conforms to a typical defined benefit plan that is mature but is sponsored by a growing firm. I incorporated retirees in the model by converting the $25 lump sum in the above multiperson firm into an indexed annuity payable until death at age eighty.[18]

The inclusion of retirees works to reduce the impact of the new limit because retiree annuities, whether flat nominal amounts or contractually indexed to inflation (as in my model), are counted as both ongoing *and* termination benefits in the Internal Revenue Code. Thus, the 50 percent cushion applied to retiree liabilities can be used to help "cushion" deficiencies in the permissible funding amounts for younger workers.

I assumed there was one retiree at each age from 65 to age 80 and two workers at each age from age 40 to 65. This distribution corresponds to the assumption of the 3:10 ratio of retirees to workers. As shown in the last column of Table 4–3, the inclusion of retirees in the model reduces the tax rate. For example, when the interest is 10 percent, the effective tax rate on defined benefit plans is 3.8 percent compared to 9.9 percent when there are no retirees.[19]

Unindexed annuities. It is important to understand that the above calculations are lower-bound estimates of the impact of the new funding rules. The reason is that, in my model, the annuity was set equal to $1.67 per year at age 65 and was contractually indexed to inflation until

TABLE 4–3 Differential Tax on Selected Defined Benefit Plans

*Interest Rate**	*One-Person Plan*	*Multiperson Plans*	
		No Retirees	*25% Retirees*
5.0	1.8	0.0	0.0
7.5	5.9	3.7	0.0
10.0	12.2	9.9	3.8
12.5	19.8	17.2	9.4
15.0	28.1	25.2	15.9

*Numbers in table are percents.

NOTE: See text for description of plan assumptions.

age 80. Recalling a real interest rate of zero, this annuity corresponds to an age-65 lump-sum equivalent value of $25. Because it was contractually guaranteed, the cost of living adjustments (COLAs) can be counted as termination benefits under the new rules.

In reality, firms almost always adjust postretirement benefits for inflation, but they do not do so contractually.[20] Instead, they award these increases on an ad hoc basis, a feature presumably related to the uncertain nature of investment returns in portfolios comprised of stocks, long-term bonds, and the like. In short, the flexibility of inflation adjustments after retirement is presumably a mechanism by which workers can share in the investment risk that characterizes the pension portfolio (see Chapter 1).

Under the old funding rules, ad hoc COLAs, even though anticipated, could not be prefunded as such. But as a practical matter, as long as the pension plan was not dominated by retirees, actuaries could effectively prefund these anticipated benefit increases by adjusting other assumptions in the funding calculation. For example, they would increase their wage growth assumption so as to increase the level of permissible funding by a sufficient amount to accommodate the plan's anticipated (though not contractual) COLA awards.

Under the new funding limits, it is not generally possible for actuaries to effectively fund for ad hoc COLA policies. The constraint is effective because most assumptions have been made irrelevant by use of a termination concept in the new rules. Thus, if the promised annuity was $1.67 starting at age 65, the old rules permitted actuaries in most plans to effectively set contribution rates that reflected ad hoc policies to provide for some COLA adjustments to retiree benefits. Under the new rules, the termination benefit is assumed to be $1.67 from age 65 to age 80 in *nominal* terms. Thus, at age 65, the present value of the annuity is valued at $12.97 (the value of a stream of nominal annuity payments of $1.67 for 15 years, discounted at 10%), not $25.

If I recalculated the above excise tax rates imposed by the new rules on defined benefit plans under the assumption that annuities are effectively but not contractually indexed to prices, all effective tax rates would be higher. For example, when the interest rate is 10 percent, the effective tax rate on defined benefit plans increases from 3.8 percent to 10.3 percent.

The only way to circumvent this constraint is to contractually promise postretirement benefits. This change would qualify the anticipated adjustments for prefunding. For all intents and purposes, however, a contractual COLA eliminates any possibility of risk-sharing in investment returns by workers. Presumably, shareholders would be willing to promise this degree of certainty only if the portfolio was invested intensely in short-term bills which exhibit little volatility in real returns.[21] The less risky portfolio, of course, would come at the expense of lower expected pension benefits.

Interest rate sensitivity. To illustrate the sensitivity of the effective excise tax levied against defined benefit plans by the new funding limits, I calculated the tax under 5 interest rates for the one-person and the multiperson plans discussed above (with contractual COLAs). The results are depicted in Table 4–3.

The results show that at a relatively low interest rate, 5 percent, the excise tax rates on all plans are negligible. At this interest rate, 150 percent times termination liabilities is almost equal to ongoing benefits at most age and service levels. For a 7.5 percent interest rate, the tax rates increase to roughly 6 and 4 percent for the one-person plan and multiperson plan with active workers of all ages but with no retirees. The implicit tax at this interest rate is still negligible for a 3:10 retiree-to-worker ratio. At a 12.5 percent interest rate, however, the tax rate in all plans becomes significant. For the relatively young plans, the effective excise tax approaches 20 percent; for the more mature plan, the tax rate is 9.4 percent. Again, if an annuity was promised that was implicitly tied to prices (but not contractually promised) and had the same lump-sum value at age 65, all these tax rates would be several percentage points higher.

Summary. In short, the new full funding limits promise to impose a tax bias against defined benefit plans. The burden is highest for plans heavily populated by active workers and for plans that award ad hoc inflation adjustments, as is the case in most plans. At relatively high interest rates, but certainly within the range of rates that have occurred in recent history, the new limits may make defined benefit plans for new firms prohibitively expensive relative to equally generous defined contribution plans.[22]

The rules also impose a bias in favor of plans that offer contractual COLAs because contractual COLAs can be funded under the new rules, but ad hoc COLA policies cannot.[23] Contractual COLAs, together with a benefit promise indexed to final wages, however, essentially imply a risk-free promise from the perspective of workers. But if workers expect a no-risk pension, they also cannot expect to share in the risk premia affiliated with a riskier portfolio and hence presumably will expect lower benefit levels. If firms, in fact, invest in risky portfolios—and I will show in the next section why they have an incentive to do so—stockholders take the gains from the higher expected returns, and workers receive a benefit that reflects the equivalent of zero-risk returns.

One public policy solution to the low-risk, low-benefit bias created by OBRA is to permit actuaries to fund for expected retirement COLAs based on experience in the plan. As long as appropriate amortization rules for incorrect assumptions are specified (see below), this rule change would not permit systematic overfunding.

SOURCES OF OVERFUNDING

The two elements that pose a conflict for pension tax policy now have been introduced. The first problem is deliberate overfunding of pension plan trust funds. The second is the distortion on behavior caused by rules designed to control overfunding. As an empirical matter, many, if not most, defined benefit pension plans are overfunded in relation to ongoing liabilities. This means that assets exceed those required to pay for pension promises based on service-to-date, accounting for indexing of benefits to final wages and at least partially to prices beyond retirement. Since, by construction, defined contribution plans cannot be overfunded, there has been an implicit tax bias in permissive funding rules in favor of defined benefit plans. Unless carefully designed, however, constraints on funding of defined benefit plans may create a tax bias in the opposite direction in favor of defined contribution plans.

To find a resolution to these problems, it is necessary to devise rules that prevent overfunding. At the same time, the rules should not bias firms' choices of either pension plan type, or asset allocation in the pension portfolio.

Illustration of Overfunding

Prior to the enactment of new funding rules in the Omnibus Budget Reconciliation Act in 1987 (OBRA), the intent of the then-existing funding rules was that plans would not have assets in excess of ongoing liabilities. However, the way in which the limit was enforced permitted systematic overfunding for long periods.

To illustrate, consider the one-person example above, in which the plan accumulated funds over 25 years, adding one dollar each year in real terms to accommodate one more year of service accruals. This scenario is depicted in Figure 4–3 by the solid horizontal line. The funded

FIGURE 4–3 Scenario for Overfunding: Pre-OBRA Rules

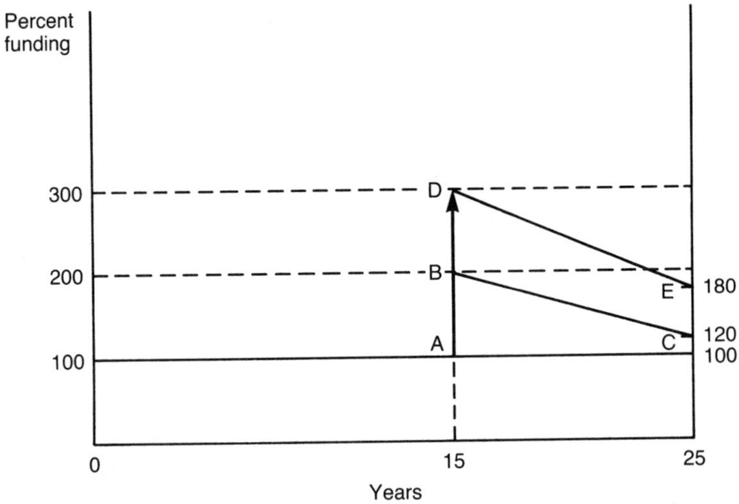

ratio is 100 percent in every year from zero to 25. In year 15, for example, assets in real terms amounted to $15; new contributions in year 16 were $1 in real terms.

Suppose that instead of holding essentially riskless assets (T-bills, in the example), the plan held securities with more volatile returns, like stocks. Suppose that in year 15 the value of the stocks doubled from $15 to $30. The plan would become 100 percent overfunded. For simplicity, assume that following the capital gain, the portfolio was switched back to all T-bills, and thus yielded a zero real rate of return over the next 10 years.

The old funding rules did not require the plan to return the extra $15 in overfunding to the plan sponsor, nor did it require the firm to pay taxes on earnings on the extra $15. Instead, the firm was required to amortize the experience gain (in this case $15) over 15 years. That is, when the firm was to make its annual "normal cost" contribution of $1 in year 16 to account for one more year of service accrual, it would be required to deduct from this the amortized value of its investment gain. In the example, the experience credit would be $1: that is, $15 in gains amortized over 15 years is $1 per year.[24] Thus, in year 16, no net contribution would be made, and the plan still would be overfunded: compare $30 in assets to $16 in liabilities.

If we follow this logic through year 25, the pension still would have $30 in assets and $25 in liabilities; the plan would be 20 percent overfunded.[25] Over the entire 10-year period following the capital gain, overfunding would have averaged 60 percent of liabilities. The funded ratio under this scenario is depicted by the schedule labelled ABC in Figure 4–3.

Had the capital gain in year 15 been $30 instead of $15, part of the overfunding *never* would have been amortized. In this case, the amortized value of the experience gain is $2 per year ($30 in experience gains amortized over 15 years). The firm would subtract the $2 amortized gain from its "normal" contribution for additional service accruals—in our example, one dollar per year. But since this offset would result in a negative contribution—that is, it implies that the plan would have to *return* monies to the firm—the code permitted the plan to retain a lower limit on net contributions of zero. In the example, this means that only $1 of each $2 in amortized gains would be used; the other $1 would never be used as a contribution offset.[26]

Since amortized *losses* could always be offset by higher contributions, there was an asymmetry in the old funding rules. Thus, in year 25, assuming the firm converted its assets into T-bills after its capital gain, it still would have $45 in assets compared to liabilities that now would amount to $25. Over the entire ten-year period, overfunding would average 140 percent of liabilities (the average funding ratio would be 240 percent). This scenario is depicted by the schedule labelled ADE in the figure.

This example is constructed to be extreme to illustrate a point, but this does not mean that, in reality, the same rules can not generate similar amounts of overfunding. The key to generating overfunding in a defined benefit plan trust fund is to hold some risky assets in the portfolio. Because of volatility in returns, chances are good that the pension plan holding, say, stocks instead of bonds in its portfolio, can get on the upside of full funding. Then the plan sponsor can take advantage of long amortization periods and the zero bound on net contributions to remain overfunded for lengthy periods of time.

To show this, I performed some simulations elsewhere.[27] I portrayed a pension plan with a balanced work force like the plan used in the tax illustrations above.[28] Liabilities were indexed so as to equal 100 in 1950; since the plan was in steady state, its liabilities in real terms remained at 100 over the entire period from 1950 to 1986. In one case, I supposed the plan held 100 percent in one-year T-bills; in the other, I supposed the plan held all stocks (in particular, an S&P-500 index). I applied the amortization rules to these plans as specified in the Internal Revenue Code.[29] I assumed that, in discounting liabilities, the actuary used an interest rate equal to the 10-year Treasury rate.[30] The balances for selected years during the simulation are portrayed in Table 4–4.

The results show that if the pension plan held one-year T-bills over the entire period, the average asset balance in the pension plan from 1951 to 1986 would have been 101, in comparison to 100 in ongoing

TABLE 4–4 Trust Balances under Pre-OBRA Rules: Treasury Bills versus Stock Portfolios

	Portfolio Composition	
Selected Years	*T-Bills*	*All Stock*
1950	100	100
1960	100	273
1970	103	336
1980	92	178
1986	108	252
Average	101	261

NOTE: Balances are expressed in 1950 dollars.

liabilities. Since one-year T-bills are not entirely riskless assets, the funded ratio showed some variance, ranging from 92 percent in 1980 to 108 percent in 1986. A portfolio comprised entirely of long-term bonds generated similar results: average funding levels were 94 percent of ongoing liabilities.

In contrast, the all-stock portfolio averaged 261 percent of liabilities. The plan was over 400 percent funded in an ongoing sense in 1969. It attained this overfunding while adhering to the old funding rules over the entire period.[31] The differences in attained funding levels between the all bond and all stock portfolios are displayed graphically in Figure 4–4.

Omnibus Budget Reconciliation Act of 1987 (OBRA)

New full funding rules were enacted by OBRA in 1987. Two additional constraints were imposed on pension plan funding. First, the 1987 legislation reduced the amortization period for experience gains and losses from 15 to 5 years. Second, instead of permitting funding of 100 percent of ongoing pension obligations, the new law permits funding up to 150 percent of termination liabilities. Contributions to the plan must be zero as long as this constraint is binding.[32] Previously, the full funding limit was defined as 100 percent of ongoing liabilities.[33]

As discussed above, the problem with the rule is that the cushion is insufficient to cover real (or ongoing) pension liabilities over some range of interest rates. For example, in the model used above, as long as the interest rate is below 8 percent, the new rule permits full funding of ongoing obligations (150% percent of termination liabilities at this interest rate is equal to or exceeds ongoing liabilities). For interest rates above this, the new rules effectively legislate underfunding. Thus, in the 1980s when long-term interest rates were in the vicinity of 12 per-

FIGURE 4–4 Funding Levels before OBRA

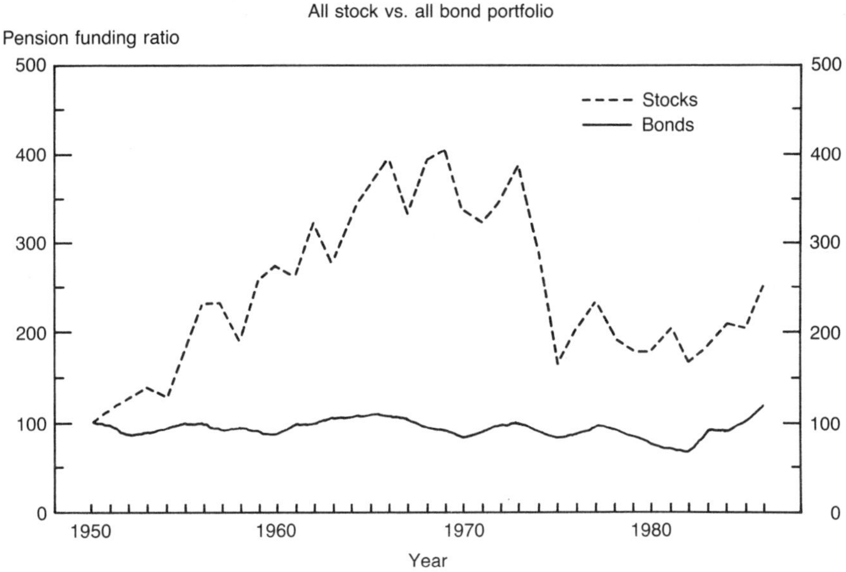

cent or more, 150 percent of termination liabilities in the model were less than 80 percent of ongoing liabilities.

Impact of the New Rules

To show the impact of the five-year amortization schedule and the 150 percent funding limit, the balances for the portfolio strategies presented in Table 4–4 were recalculated under the new rules. For purposes of the calculations, I assumed that the new law was effective on January 1, 1951. The results of the simulations are shown in Table 4–5.

The results show that the impact of the legislation depends largely on the nature of the pension portfolio. The all T-bill portfolio exhibits only small experience gains or losses over the period and thus essentially is unaffected by faster amortization. It is affected, however, by the new 150 percent funding rules whenever the new limit falls below 100. Because the new limits were not constraining until the late 1970s (prior to this time, interest rates were sufficiently low so that 150 percent of termination liabilities exceeded ongoing liabilities), the overall portfolio balances for the entire period are not substantially affected.

TABLE 4–5 Trust Balances under Post-OBRA Rules

	Portfolio Composition	
Selected Years	*T-Bills*	*All Stock*
1950	100	100
1960	101	273
1970	101	336
1980	88	178
1986	74	252
Average	94	261
Pre-OBRA	101	261

NOTE: Balances are expressed in 1950 dollars.

The impression changes if funding levels attained towards the end of the period are studied. The funding level in 1986 was 74 percent compared to 108 percent under the old funding limits (see Table 4–4). If the interest rate remained in the vicinity of 12 percent into the indefinite future (the prevailing interest rate in the simulations in the early 1980s), trust balances in these portfolios would settle to roughly 75 percent of ongoing liabilities. This merely illustrates the point made above that if the plan invests in riskless assets, it essentially is required to maintain an underfunded plan which creates a tax bias in favor of defined contribution plans. The differences in funding levels in the all T-bill portfolio using the pre- and post-OBRA funding rules are displayed graphically in Figure 4–5.

In contrast, the all stock portfolio strategy in the simulation is completely unaffected by the new legislation. The all stock portfolio balance averages 261 percent of ongoing liabilities under either the pre- or post-OBRA funding rules. The impact is zero in this case because capital gains in the stock portfolio are so substantial over the period relative to the interest rate used to discount liabilities (which is tied to bond yields), that the simulated pension plan was against the zero-contribution limit in virtually all years under the old rules. Thus, in this case, the new contribution and funding constraints are entirely redundant.

In summary, the new OBRA maximum funding rules have two effects. First, for firms and workers that wish to use low-risk assets to back the pension promise, the new rules impose a tax bias in favor of defined contribution plans. Second, the rules retain the incentive to hold risky assets in the pension fund. When expected tax benefits from overfunding are higher, more risk is undertaken by the pension fund. Whether the inclusion of more risk in the pension fund affects pension benefits depends upon whether the trust fund is viewed as entirely separate from the plan sponsor.

FIGURE 4–5 Impact of OBRA

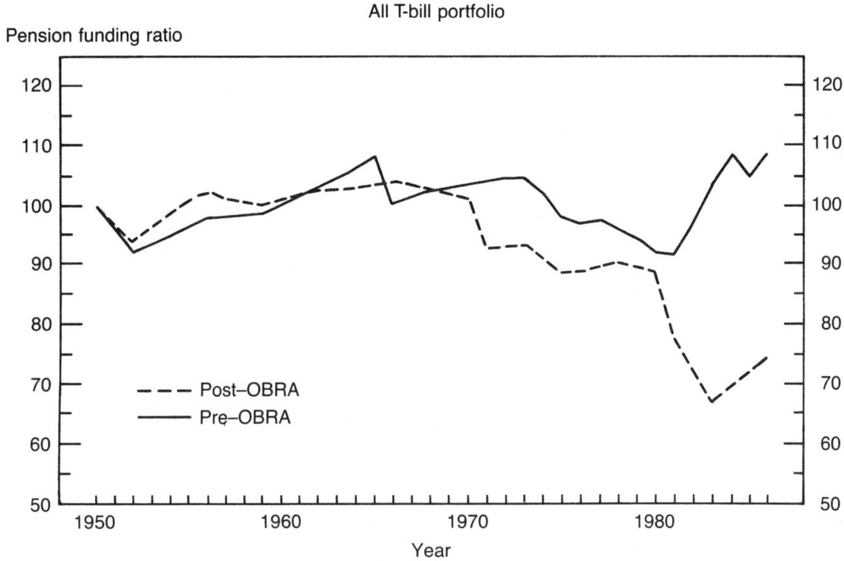

On the one hand, if the pension promise is backed by assets in the *firm* (not just those in the pension trust), then as long as the overall risk level in the firm is unaffected, the firm's implicit guarantee of the pension is unaffected. The only short-term loser from the risky strategy is the U.S. Treasury. In the long run, however, as Congress works to redress persistent overfunding, more funding constraints and therefore more distortions are predictable.

On the other hand, if the firm is unwilling to guarantee all pension losses with assets in the firm, the impact of the new law potentially is more important. Suppose pension trusts are viewed as assets separate from the firm, and these assets alone implicitly back the pension promise. The new law provides a tax incentive to engage in a riskier portfolio strategy. If a low-risk strategy is adopted and long-term interest rates are 10 percent, roughly 75 percent of liabilities can accumulate in a tax-free trust. Full funding is attainable only if a riskier portfolio strategy is followed. If the downside of the riskier strategy is realized (i.e., large capital losses), the likelihood increases that some pension promises will be unfulfilled.[34]

If Congress wishes to eliminate overfunding and retain a neutral influence over the choice of pension plan and type of portfolio, it must develop funding rules that create a reasonable relation between ongoing pension liabilities and pension assets, regardless of the composition of the pension portfolio. I have outlined an alternative approach to this problem in the next section.

AN ALTERNATE APPROACH TO ENFORCE FULL FUNDING

The intent of Congress apparently is to extend the consumption tax concept to defined benefit plans but to prevent stockholders from taking advantage of this by "oversaving" in these trusts through various portfolio risk strategies. In this section, I will consider a mechanism that permits Congress to frustrate firms' overfunding strategies without affecting their ability to fully fund their plans on an ongoing basis.

First, suppose plans were permitted to fund for ongoing benefits. Essentially, termination benefits are an irrelevancy to the economic value of pensions as viewed by workers and firms and, as such, funding limits tied to the termination concept are a formula for creating significant distortions in the pension market. Second, the five-year amortization period for experience gains and losses should be retained. Lengthy amortization periods work to generate smoother contribution flows to the plan but permit overfunding to persist for long periods of time. A five-year rule largely eliminates this potential but, at the same time, permits some smoothing of gains and losses over short periods of time.

Third, *all* investment gains (what actuaries call experience gains) should be applied in full against normal (service accrual) contributions. *If amortized experience gains exceed normal contributions, the surplus is transferred to the firm and treated as taxable income.* We can refer to this as the introduction of a *symmetry principle* into the funding rules because all losses and *all gains* are amortized in full.

For example, consider the one-person plan developed above. Recall the instance where in year 15, assets increased in value from 15 to 30 dollars. Under the old rules, this meant that one dollar of this gain was amortized each year, exactly offsetting the normal contribution also equal to one dollar per year. In the above proposal, the $15 gain would be amortized over five years, or $3 per year. Since this amount exceeds the one dollar "normal" contribution, the plan would return $2 to the firm in each of the ensuing five years to be included in taxable income at the corporate level. If no additional capital gains or losses occurred, the plan's funding level would return to 100 percent of liabilities after five years.

To demonstrate the impact of this policy, I reran the simulation model above, imposing the proposed rules as if they were in effect on January 1, 1951. The results, demonstrated in Table 4–6, show that the rules are successful in generating trust balances that are reasonably related to ongoing liabilities. The all-stock portfolio balance is reduced from 161 percent overfunded on average under the OBRA rules to 29 percent under the alternative rules. The all T-bill portfolio averages 101

TABLE 4–6 Trust Balances under a Symmetrical Funding Rule

	Portfolio Composition	
Selected Years	*T-Bills*	*All Stock*
1950	100	100
1960	101	134
1970	101	96
1980	96	100
1986	110	140
Average	102	129
Post-OBRA	94	261
Pre-OBRA	101	261

NOTE: Balances are expressed in 1950 dollars.

percent and is within 10 percent of full funding over all years. While there is still some bias in favor of risky strategies, the bias is small compared to either the pre- or post-OBRA rules.

If these rules were effected, the funding limits enacted in the Omnibus Budget Reconciliation Act should be repealed. The result would be that overfunding in defined benefit plans would be substantially contained. In addition, the rules would not seriously bias firms in favor of either defined benefit or defined contribution plans and would not distort choices in favor of risky portfolios in defined benefit plans.

DISTORTIONS FROM DIFFERENT TAX TREATMENT OF STOCKS AND BONDS

As a final matter, I will address the problems created by different tax treatment of stocks and bonds. Historically, these securities effectively have been taxed differently, owing to lower tax rates on capital gains. In the past, this difference created an opportunity for stockholders to "abuse" the use of the tax-exempt pension fund without overfunding. Although this problem has been largely eliminated by removing the capital gains tax in the Tax Reform Act of 1986,[35] we need to understand this problem because it will be recreated if favorable tax treatment towards capital gains is reinstituted at some future date.

To isolate this phenomenon, let us consider a very simple model that captures the essence of the problem but does not create unnecessary complications. I will discuss issues surrounding the optimal asset allocation in the pension under pre-1986 tax law. In particular, suppose there is no corporate income tax. The personal tax rate is 33 percent, but the tax applies only to earnings from bonds, not from stock (this mimics past preferential income tax treatment towards earnings from stock without introducing undue complications). Other things constant, suppose workers prefer a balanced portfolio in the pension because it gives them the desired trade-off between risk and required implicit contributions (see Chapter 1). Thus, the pension holds 50 in stocks and 50 in bonds. Suppose stockholders who own the firm also hold 50 in stock and 50 in bonds in their personal portfolios.

Prior to the Tax Reform Act of 1986, because of preferential tax treatment of stock, in equilibrium, the *gross-of-tax* return on bonds should have exceeded the risk-adjusted return on stock. That is, if both securities were to pay a risk-adjusted return of 10 percent, the after-tax return would be 6.7 percent on bonds and 10 percent on stock (recall that in the illustration, the assumed tax on stock earnings is zero, which serves to mimic the substantial advantage awarded to stocks relative to bonds prior to 1986). This situation would create an excess demand for stock and an excess supply of bonds. Equilibrium would be attained when the *net-of-tax* risk-adjusted returns were equal. Suppose this equilibrium occurred in a situation where the before-tax return on bonds was 12 percent; and after-tax, was 8 percent (that is, 12 percent gross return, minus the 33 percent personal tax). The before- and after- (risk-adjusted) return on stock also is 8 percent.

Total tax revenue on the 100 in stocks and 100 in bonds held by the pension plan and stockholders in the example is easy to determine. The pension trust is tax exempt, and, thus, no tax revenue is expected. Stockholders' portfolios are outside the trust and thus are exposed to taxation. Since 50 of their holdings are in stocks, the earnings of which are tax exempt in the example, no taxes are collectable on these securities. But earnings on bonds are taxable. Taxable interest from all bonds held by stockholders amounts to the 12 percent interest rate, times 50, or six units of taxable income per year. Tax revenue amounts to 33 percent of this, or two units per year.

This estimate, however, greatly overstates tax revenue to the U.S. Treasury. Stockholders effectively can make an implicit contract with workers. Stockholders will put 100 percent of the pension trust fund in bonds but pay benefits based on expected returns from a 50 to 50 stock-bond portfolio.[36] Stockholders will hold 100 percent stock but their long-term return implicitly will be tied to a 50 to 50 stock-bond portfolio. In effect, stockholders switch their 50 in bonds with 50 in stock from the pension fund. Pension benefits are unchanged.

The effect of this transaction is that tax revenue from these workers and stockholders is now zero. The tax-exempt trust fund would hold all the taxable securities (bonds), and taxpaying stockholders would hold all the tax-favored securities (stock). This switch is referred to as a *tax-arbitrage* transaction and is the basis for past prescriptions for pension plans to hold (but not necessarily base benefits on) all-bond portfolios.[37] Nothing real happens. The only loser is the U.S. Treasury. Stockholders and workers save a flow of two units of income per year to share somehow amongst themselves—an amount that otherwise would have been sent to the U.S. Treasury.

While ERISA technically requires that the pension plan trust be used for the exclusive benefit of participants, as a practical matter, there is no way the tax-arbitrage strategy could be detected, and, thus, there is no way for the Congress to contain the tax loss that would result. As a general principle, if the Congress gives tax-exempt status to pension plans and also applies different tax treatment to different types of securities, it is inevitable that firms will engage in an arbitrage scheme to increase the combined tax benefits of both tax policies.

In the Tax Reform Act of 1986, the Congress eliminated the special capital gains tax preference and thus put stock and bond returns more or less on the same tax basis.[38] In so doing, it eliminated the incentive for firms to distort their pension plan portfolios to engage in tax arbitrage. If this tax principle is retained and if funding rules are modified as discussed above, the government will finally be out of the business of influencing the portfolio composition of pension plans trusts.[39] If the special capital gains tax treatment is reintroduced, however, a mechanism will be set up that permits tax arbitrage in a way that is virtually impossible to prevent.

SUMMARY AND CONCLUSIONS

In a tax system that generally taxes capital income, the provision for special tax-free accumulation vehicles creates incentives for their overuse. Congressional intent to limit the tax exemption is frustrated by rational taxpayers. This gives rise to legislation like the Omnibus Budget Reconciliation Act that is intended to limit tax abuse.

The problem with this type of ad hoc legislation is that it may work to create even more tax bias. The law, in effect, provides a tax incentive in favor of defined contribution plans or defined benefit plans with risky portfolios. A more effective public policy—and one more consistent with a neutral government policy towards pensions—is to redress the overfunding problem without, at the same time interfering with the optimal free market choice of type of plan and portfolio composition.

One way to accomplish this is to return to the full funding limit that applied prior to 1987. This policy ensures a rational relation between funding levels and real levels of workers' savings for retirement. To prevent overfunding, relatively short amortization periods for experience gains and losses can be imposed (the new five-year period enacted in 1987 could be retained), and full application of these amounts against normal contributions can be applied, even if this means that sometimes plans will refund monies to plan sponsors (to be included in taxable corporate income).[40]

These proposals, together with recent legislation to repeal the capital gains tax, would substantially reduce the government's influence on pension portfolio decisions. In combination with proposals discussed in previous chapters, the stage would be set for a more neutral pension tax policy in the United States. The next chapter will bring all these proposals together to describe this policy in its entirety.

ENDNOTES

1. The data are taken from the Form 5500 Annual Pension Plan Reports submitted to the Internal Revenue Service each year. Data for 1986 are estimates based on information reported in Wyatt & Co., *Survey of Actuarial Assumptions and Funding* (Washington, D.C., 1987).
2. I use a discount rate equal to 2 percent for all liabilities including those affiliated with current retirees. This assumes substantial ad hoc indexing during retirement. For more detail on this discounting technique, see R. Ippolito, *Pensions, Economics, and Public Policy,* Chapters 3 and 4.
3. During this period, funding ratios in defined benefit plans fell on average by 34 percentage points. See R. Ippolito and W. Kolodrubetz (eds.), *The Handbook of Pension Statistics*, p. 461.
4. For this calculation, I approximated these liabilities by using the average assumed actuarial interest rate of 7.7 percent in the 1984 5500 Forms for retirees and a 3 percent net discount rate (interest rate minus wage projection) for active participants.
5. Similar results are found using the 1986 Form 5500 data.
6. The new rules also generate an extraordinary but temporary increase in tax revenue because during the few years it takes for overfunded plans to defund sufficiently to meet the new limit, tax-deductible contributions to plans will be reduced, thereby increasing taxable corporate income. The long-run impact is a lower level of assets held in tax-exempt trusts, thereby increasing the income tax base to include more capital earnings.
7. This assumes that no unanticipated events occurred over the funding period. For example, if investment returns were not zero in real terms as assumed, or if wages increased or decreased over time in real terms (compared to the zero-wage-growth assumption), the consequent changes in the liability calculations would result in amortized additions or subtractions to the so-called normal contribution.
8. Overfunding triggered gradual amortization of excess assets against normal contributions made to the plan.
9. When this constraint is violated, no additional contributions to the plan are permitted.
10. Increases in real wages, owing to more seniority in the firm and economy-wide increases in productivity, also work to increase pension benefits at retirement.
11. Some of these assumptions include the interest rate, expected wage growth, the likelihood of workers quitting before retirement, and the expected retirement age.
12. The U.S. Treasury requires use of an interest rate between 90 and 110 percent of the weighted 4-year average of 30-year Treasury bond rates.
13. That is,

$$PVT(1,0) \times 150\% = 10\% \times 1 \text{ year} \times \$10e^{-.10(25)} \times 150\%$$

$$= \$0.123.$$

Termination liabilities in this equation are similar to ongoing liabilities calculated in Chapter 1 (see equation in footnote 10). Both recognize that the pension liability after one year of service equals the 10 percent generosity factor, times one year of service, times current wage, \$10. But unlike the ongoing calculation, the 10 percent salary projection factor is missing in the termination calculation.

14. See discussion in Chapter 1.
15. That is,

$$\text{PVT}(15,0) \times 150\% = 10\% \times 15 \text{ years} \times \$10e^{-.10(10)} \times 150\%$$
$$= \$8.27.$$

16. Assuming that the interest rate and the expected wage growth rate are each 10 percent, the calculation of ongoing benefits is depicted by:

$$\text{PVO} = \int_{a=0}^{25} 10\% \times a \text{ years} \times \$10 \, da.$$

The solution to this expression is \$312.

17. That is, 150 percent of termination liabilities are denoted as follows:

$$\text{PVT} \times 150\% = 150\% \times \int_{a=0}^{25} 10\% \times a \text{ years} \times \$10 \times e^{-.10(25-a)} \, da.$$

The solution to this expression is \$237.

18. Had I converted the \$25 lump sum into an unindexed annuity with the same present value at age 65, the results would not be altered.
19. As in the other plans, the tax rate is expressed as the extra tax assessed, divided by the lump-sum equivalent (\$25 per retiree) paid to the two annual retirees from the plan.
20. Most large pension plans make ad hoc inflation adjustments after retirement; few plans offer contractual cost-of-living adjustments. See R. Clark, "Postretirement Adjustments."
21. For an application of this principle to a guaranteed insurance contract, see R. Ippolito, *The Economics of Pension Insurance*, Chapter 10.
22. In this context, I define generosity in an ex ante sense: the flow of expected contributions to both plans is identical. After the fact, it might turn out that the defined contribution plan has higher or lower value than its defined benefit counterpart.
23. Under the old rules, funding for ad hoc COLAs technically was not allowed but was effectively done in practice through adjustments of other actuarial assumptions.
24. In reality, the amortization of the experience gain is done in flat nominal dollars over 15 years.
25. The plan also likely would have been constrained by the full funding limit in the Internal Revenue Code (Section 412). This limit precludes contributions to the plan if actuarial assets exceed actuarial liabilities plus one year of normal contributions.
26. The rules did not require that unused gains be carried forward.
27. See Richard A. Ippolito, "The Role of Risk in a Tax Arbitrage Pension Portfolio," *Financial Analysts Journal* (1990), forthcoming.
28. In particular, the plan had one worker at each age over a 25-year span of preretirement ages. There were no retirees. The pension benefit was given in the form

of a lump sum equal to 10 percent, times years of service, times final wage. Real wage growth and the real interest rate were zero.

29. These included both the amortization rules and full funding limit in Section 412 of the Code.

30. In the simulation, in steady state, "normal" contributions (contributions unaffected by experience gains or losses) were 10 percent of liabilities, and benefit payouts also equaled 10 percent. This is typical of pension plans in the United States.

31. The fact that plans have not usually been 400 percent funded does not mean that the model is wrong. Prior to the Tax Reform Act of 1986, it was advantageous for pensions and other tax-exempt entities to hold bonds in the portfolio. See Fisher Black, "The Tax Consequences of Long-Run Pension Policy," *Financial Analysts Journal* 36 (July–August 1980), pp. 3–10; and Irwin Tepper, "Taxation and Corporate Pension Policy," *Journal of Finance* (March 1981), pp. 1–14. The optimal policy was to hold some portion of bonds and equity to take advantage of all features of the tax code favoring pension plans. See discussion below. In addition to providing a means to exploit funding rules, stocks might also have affected overfunding if actuaries' choices of discount rates were influenced by the asset allocation on the pension. See M. Scholes and M. Wolfson, *Taxes and Business Strategy: A Global Planning Approach* (Prentice-Hall, 1989).

32. Once plans fall under the 150 percent constraint, the old funding rules prevail (except for those plans less than 100 percent funded on a termination basis; these plans are subject to a special set of accelerated funding rules).

33. See note 24.

34. ERISA does not permit firms to reduce nominal benefits accrued to date, but the firm can otherwise reduce real benefits by awarding fewer postretirement ad hoc inflation adjustments; reducing the generosity parameter for future service accruals; or in the extreme, terminating the pension plan and paying off termination benefits as required by law.

35. The bias has not been entirely eliminated because capital gains on stock are not subject to taxation until they are realized.

36. See discussion of the relation between benefits and risk in the portfolio in Chapter 1.

37. For more detail on how the pension tax-arbitrage game works, see F. Black, "The Tax Consequences," and I. Tepper, "Taxation and Corporate Pension Policy."

38. There is still some advantage imparted to stocks because tax is not assessed until the gains are realized.

39. ERISA itself does not constrain pension plan portfolios except to restrict holdings of the plan sponsor's own securities beyond 10 percent of assets (except in stock-bonus defined contribution plans) and to require diversification across many securities; certainly, an all bond or all S&P stock portfolio is permissible under the regulation.

40. While, in principle, the short amortization period and the symmetry funding principle were illustrated in the context of controlling underfunding stemming from investment gains, the same rules would protect against all sources of overfunding. For example, if actuaries assume unrealistically high wage growth or low quit rates to overstate ongoing pension liabilities, the same amortization rule and symmetry principle would also ensure that overfunding from these sources would be short-lived.

CHAPTER 5

Pension Tax Policy: A Summing Up

BASIC PRINCIPLES

This monograph has covered much material, so it is useful to recap some of the more important issues and bring together the various policy conclusions and proposals for an efficient tax policy for the United States. There is much in the pension system that is complex, some of which is attributable to a vast regulatory machinery that has been built around the pension industry. In their essence, however, pension plans, whether firm-offered defined contribution or defined benefit plans or individual retirement accounts, merely represent vehicles for workers to set aside part of their wages during their worklife to help finance consumption during retirement.

The fundamental principle that lay behind pension tax policy—in particular the tax-exempt character of pension trust funds—is that wages are taxed only once, whether these wages are used to finance immediate consumption or consumption during retirement. If it were not for this provision in tax law, wages used to finance immediate consumption would be taxed at the marginal rate as specified in the Internal Revenue Code. If used to finance consumption during retirement, wages would be assessed a so-called second tax. One tax is levied when wages are earned. A second tax is levied in a series of assessments against interest earnings as workers try to translate today's dollars into tomorrow's dollars.

The double tax amounts to a large increase in the income tax assessed on wages, but only if they are used to finance deferred consumption. For example, in Chapter 2, I demonstrated that when the interest rate is 10 percent, a 50-year-old worker, normally assessed a 15 percent income tax rate on earnings used to support immediate consumption, would pay an effective tax rate of 32 percent if earnings were saved in a tax-exposed vehicle for consumption at age 65. The imposition of the higher tax would almost surely result in workers retiring at later ages, enjoying lower standards of living during retirement and reducing the length of the work week during working years, all in reaction to an artificially higher price set by the government on retirement consumption. These distortions would take individuals away from their optimal combinations of work and leisure and reduce productivity in firms, thereby imposing economic costs of nontrivial magnitudes on the U.S. economy.

RETIREMENT DECISIONS

Pension tax policy eliminates the double tax on savings for retirement and, in so doing, removes artificial distortions from retirement decisions that otherwise would depend only on worker preferences and productivity. In this sense, the basic elements of pension tax policy reflect the principles of *neutrality*: they work in the direction of keeping the federal government out of the business of influencing retirement savings and consumption behavior that ought to be determined in the private market.

It turns out that the neutrality theme has been extended to the social security system. In major changes to the system in 1977 and 1983, Congress enacted new rules to eliminate social security from playing a major role in influencing retirement behavior. Before these changes, the system exerted large penalties on individuals who worked past age 65, and, at the same time, provided strong penalties on those retiring at ages much earlier than age 65. In 1977, the penalties imposed on early retirement were eliminated and, in 1983, a policy was effected that gradually will eliminate the penalty on delayed retirement past age 65 by the year 2005.[1] The underlying tax policy towards social security, however, still imposes a bias in favor of too much retirement.

This bias occurs because one half of social security contributions are subject to tax, but the second half is never taxed except insofar as taxable income (including tax-exempt interest) exceeds $25,000 or $32,000 for individuals and married couples. Thus, a subtle distortion is introduced into the tax code in favor of the social security system. Earnings contributed to this system are taxed at lower effective income tax rates than either earnings devoted to immediate consumption or saved through pensions for retirement. This problem, however, was addressed in 1983.

The 1983 Social Security Amendments put into motion a schedule that ultimately will tax the "second half" of social security benefits, eliminating the bias in the system favoring retirement consumption over immediate consumption. Congress did this by deliberately not indexing the taxable income threshold amounts, thereby leading to the ultimate erosion of these amounts. In the long run, virtually all wage earnings set aside to fund the social security system will be taxed once (half when contributions are made and half when benefits are taken), thereby approximating the tax policy applied towards private pensions.

Thus, taken together, pension tax policy and social security policy have made the federal government a more neutral player in future retirement decisions. There is, in these systems, however, one inconsistency which could easily be fixed. Because of progression in the income tax formula, wages saved through pensions for retirement are more likely taxed at lower rates than those paid during work years. This sets up an artificial incentive in the direction of too much retirement and too little work. This anomaly can be eliminated either by assessing taxes on pension income at marginal rates that characterize working years or assessing taxes at the time contributions are made rather than when benefits are taken.

The latter option would raise the same present value tax revenue as the former, but would be practical only for defined contribution plans and individual retirement accounts, not defined benefit plans.[2] Either of these adjustments would eliminate the so-called smoothing effect in pension tax policy. To keep the systems parallel, taxable social security benefits also must be taxed at rates that characterize those paid during working years.

DEFINED BENEFIT VERSUS DEFINED CONTRIBUTION PLANS

In addition to influencing retirement decisions directly, tax policy can also influence the types of pension plans that cover workers. The issue is important because, as discussed in Chapter 1, the two basic types of pension plans have different attributes and can have important effects on workers' well-being and overall productivity. Defined contribution plans are akin to tax-preferred savings accounts: they provide less opportunity for workers to hedge against poor investment performance and usually do not provide for annuities free of selection bias. Firms have less opportunity in these plans to encourage both long term tenure in the firm and retirement during predetermined age ranges. Thus, if pension tax policy is written so as to artificially assess higher taxes against defined benefit plans, economic inefficiencies are predictable.

In 1987, in the Omnibus Budget Reconciliation Act (OBRA), Congress enacted legislation that had precisely this effect. By rewriting pension funding laws, Congress effectively assessed an excise tax of sorts on most defined benefit plans, particularly those sponsored by firms populated by young to middle-age workers. These taxes are currently in the range of 10 to 12 percent of benefit payouts for these firms but could increase to the range of 20 percent if interest rates were to reattain levels that prevailed in the late 1970s and early 1980s.

One justification for the new rules is the inability of the previous Internal Revenue Code provisions to prevent persistent overfunding of promised benefits. The OBRA rules abandon the concept of funding for ongoing benefits and instead set limits tied to termination benefits. As long as trust funds invest primarily in low-risk assets, the rules will lead to lower funding levels in pension plans and will cause substantial underfunding on an ongoing basis for many plans.

It is not obvious, however, that this approach will be successful if pension portfolios invest more heavily in riskier assets. Simulations of pension funding under the new policy over lengthy periods of time show that by holding risky assets in the pension portfolio, the firm can generated substantial overfunding even under the new rules. What the new rules likely will be successful in accomplishing is encouraging the use of defined contribution plans and riskier portfolio strategies.[3]

One solution to the overfunding problem is to return to the principle of funding for ongoing benefits. Worker savings are reflected in ongoing benefits, not termination benefits.[4] Instead, the maximum funding rules should be revamped to prevent systematic and persistent overfunding. The new shorter amortization periods for investment gains and losses (it is now 5 instead of 15 years) ought to be retained. This provision alone, however, will not work. The law also must require *all* these amortized amounts to be applied in full against "normal" contributions to the plan, even if this means refunding some contributions to the firm (to be treated as ordinary taxable income). The effects of all erroneous actuarial assumptions, not just those reflecting investment returns, should be amortized in the same way.[5]

The net effect of this rule is to control overfunding in defined benefit pension plans without imposing an artificial tax bias that affects the choice of type of plan and the level of risk in pension plan portfolios. With these rules put in place, the government would substantially reduce its influence over both the type of pension plan offered by firms and the composition of pension portfolios.[6]

FIRM-OFFERED PENSIONS VERSUS IRAs

The above changes in pension policy would impose similar treatment on pension plans with different incentives and portfolios, but they would not award equitable treatment to pension plans offered by financial institutions. One of the most far-reaching and costly aspects of current pension tax policy is the availability of tax-exempt status exclusively for firm-offered pension plans. Individual retirement accounts are available in amounts up to less than 10 percent of permissible contributions to defined contribution plans and, for workers already covered by a pension plan, the tax provisions are less generous than those afforded pension plans.

The "preference principle" itself would not be operationally important if it were not for the so-called discrimination rules enacted by Congress in 1942. These rules make it difficult for the firm to offer different pension plans to different groups of its work force, unless the groups are comprised of similar mixes of high- and low-wage workers.[7] By imposing a one-plan-for-all rule regardless of wage level, Congress apparently intended to limit the use of pensions by high-income workers, force low-income workers to save more for retirement, and effect off-budget transfers from high- to low-income workers.

While the original motivations may have had validity in 1942, they are now outdated. Most importantly, a large, universal social security system, begun in 1935 and still in its infancy in 1942, has grown into a major source of retirement income, particularly for low-income workers. These workers receive age-65 replacement rates up to 100 percent of their wages, and there is a deliberate subsidy built into the system from high- to low-income workers. The pension system covers only a small portion of low-income workers. For those covered, the combination of social security and pension annuities generate extraordinary replacement rates which, in turn, encourage premature retirement from the work force.

In addition, perhaps in 1942, control of "overuse" of pensions by high-income workers could have been accomplished only indirectly through artificial constraints on pension plans. Clearly, this is not efficient today. Pension limits can be enforced directly by routine electronic monitoring of individual tax returns during retirement years. Limits on allowable annuities ($112,500 per year, indexed to prices[8]) have obviated the need for indirect limitations imposed by discrimination rules.

While the original purposes of the 1942 rules are now satisfied by the social security system and new technology to monitor tax returns, the rules themselves have not been repealed. This is unfortunate because the efficacy of the discrimination rules appears to be the only rationale for retaining the preference in pension tax policy for firm-sponsored pension plans. This preference principle provides strong incentives to save for retirement through firms, and essentially requires firms to offer pension plans to be competitive in labor markets. If financial institutions could offer competing pension plan vehicles directly, workers might not entrust their retirement monies with many firms now providing pensions.

A tax policy that, for all intents and purposes, requires the worker-firm savings relation, inevitably creates potential agency problems. If workers are forced to entrust their retirement savings to firms that otherwise might not be chosen in a free market to be custodians for workers' funds, then arguably it behooves the government to police the agents for potential abuse. This policing function has taken the form of regulatory machinery created largely by the Employee Retirement Income Security Act of 1974 (ERISA). ERISA controls the operation of pension plans, including reporting and disclosure rules, vesting and participation rules, minimum funding rules, as well as mandatory pension insurance coverage through a government agency.

Ironically, the data suggest that pension fraud[9] was never an important problem prior to 1974, and, even if it was, the regulations are written in such a way as to be ineffective in preventing firms that are intent on cheating workers out of most of their pension savings.[10] Instead, the law has been effective in transferring billions of dollars from workers in well-funded, healthy firms to a minority of primarily high-wage, unionized workers in dying industries who are covered by extraordinarily generous pensions. In addition, owing to the moral hazards it creates, the insurance is likely to invite more pension terminations than otherwise would occur.

The easiest way to deregulate pensions is to eliminate the preference in pension tax law for firm-sponsored pension plans: that is, to afford individual retirement accounts the same tax treatment as firm-sponsored pensions. Contributions to pension plans and IRAs should be unconstrained. The control of "overuse" of pensions should and can be controlled by enforcing the limits on annual payouts during retirement as enacted in the Tax Reform Act of 1986. Limits on each pension plan are redundant, increase the regulatory cost of pensions, and potentially distort workers' and firms' choices of pension plan and optimal savings patterns.[11] The availability of unlimited IRAs would alter the combination of vehicles used to save retirement monies, but not necessarily alter total savings.

To be sure, the new rules would change savings rates for some individuals. Under current tax law, most workers in a firm are forced to have virtually the same savings rate, regardless of differences in desired savings rates. In a free market, some workers undoubtedly would choose to save more and others less. Similarly, most workers in the firm are now required to be subject to the same penalties for quitting and the same costs of retiring from the firm at older ages. Under a policy that permitted IRAs to compete directly with pension plans, firm-sponsored pensions would survive only if they offered substantial productivity advantages. Otherwise, workers would save for retirement in the amounts and in the types of vehicles that suited their own preferences.

To let pension plans fairly compete with IRAs, most regulations on firm-offered pensions should be repealed. Firms should be permitted to use the plans they prefer, using whatever rules and combinations of incentives and types of plan that maximize productivity accounting for workers' preferences. Competition among firms would ensure that only the most efficient pension plans would survive the market test.

If workers had free choice to use either IRAs or pension plans to save for retirement, the need for government to regulate the potential agency problem the government itself created would be difficult to justify. Presumably, in a free market, the only firms left offering pensions would be those with sufficient reputations to overcome workers' concerns of retirement income security. The government could retain fiduciary regulations of pension plan sponsors akin to regulations applied against financial institutions offering IRAs—like banks, investment companies, and insurance firms.

Similarly, there would be no reason to require pension insurance coverage. If workers remaining in pension plans under a free-market system wanted insurance protection, there is no reason to believe that such protection would not arise in the private market. As a last resort, if Congress insisted on continued mandatory insurance, the guarantee levels under the insurance should be reduced dramatically. Low- to middle-income workers should not be required to pay for extraordinary benefit levels to high-wage workers as is currently done.[12]

All of the proposals made above are summarized in Table 5–1. If all these policies were effected (many, of course, are already in place), the net outcome would be that the government would retain little direct influence on individuals' choices of retirement age, retirement savings, retirement consumption, types of pension plans, composition of pension plan portfolios, and incentive effects of pensions. These policies would greatly reduce the indirect efficiency costs of current policy, as well as the direct regulatory costs. The continuation of the social security system would ensure minimum retirement consumption for all workers and prevent "spenders" from taking advantage of "savers." Otherwise, retirement decisions and all pension decisions would be made in a private market, dependent only on worker preferences and labor productivity.

APPLICATION TO RETIREE HEALTH BENEFITS

While this volume has addressed only savings for retirement, the arguments used to justify application of the consumption tax principle to pensions can equally well be used to justify a one-tax principle to all postponed consumption. I have side-stepped this issue because, while it makes economic sense to move in the direction of a consumption tax, such a move has revenue implications, the solution to which would take us far beyond the subject of this volume. It is equally important, however, to recognize illegitimate applications of the pension tax principle to all retirement savings, including those used to pur-

TABLE 5–1 Towards a Neutral Pension Tax Policy

Category	*Current*	*Proposal*
Basic Tax Policy		
Contribution deduction	Yes	Retain
Tax-exempt trust	Yes	Retain up to 100% of ongoing benefits; either • impose better funding rules (5-year amortization and symmetry); • or treat earnings on excess assets as taxable corporate income.
Tax deferral	Benefits taxed at rates during retirement.	Retain but eliminate income smoothing: • tax benefits at rates paid during work years or • tax contributions (more feasible in defined contribution plans).
Social Security		
Penalty for work after age 65	To be gradually eliminated by the year 2005.	Retain
Penalty for early retirement	Essentially eliminated in 1977.	Retain
Tax policy	Tax 50% of contributions; tax 50% of benefits if taxable income exceeds $25,000 or $32,000 (couple) but freeze thresholds at current nominal levels to gradually erode with inflation.	Retain or accelerate erosion of thresholds.
Related Issues		
Vehicles eligible for tax-exempt accumulation	Firm-offered plans only (with inconsequential exceptions).	Expand to IRAs (subject to same limits as def. cont. plans).
Payout limit	$112,500 per year during retirement, including all tax deferred income (except social security benefits).	Retain
Tax qualification rules	Discrimination rules, integration rules, antibackloading rules.	Eliminate
Contribution limits	$30,000 for DC plans, $90,000 projected benefits for DB plans.	Eliminate (redundant to payout limits).
Agency regulation	Vesting, participation, minimum funding.	Eliminate
	Mandatory insurance	Make voluntary or retain at minimal levels.
	Fiduciary regulations	Retain

chase retiree health benefits. This issue is so closely related to the tax and pension issues addressed above that it requires some attention, particularly since it is an issue currently in the midst of some policy debate.

In particular, an issue parallel to pension payments is the practice of firms offering health insurance policies to retirees as part of the retirement package. These policies cover workers until they are entitled to Medicare at age 65 and often supplement this coverage after 65. These health programs can be viewed in a similar way to pensions. They represent implicit savings by workers for a supplemental retirement benefit beyond the direct payment of pensions.

Retirement health benefits, however, are *not* treated like pension benefits in the tax code. Tax-exempt trust accounts are not availed to corporations to accumulate implicit worker contribution for health insurance coverage during retirement. Because of the apparently obvious parallel in the two schemes, a common policy prescription is to extend pension tax policy to retiree health benefits. The parallel, however, is apparent, not real.

In the case of pensions, earnings saved to finance consumption during retirement are taxed once at the time they are received as benefits. According to the symmetry property of the consumption tax, as long as tax rates assessed against benefits are equal to those faced during working years (when contributions are made), this practice is analytically equivalent to taxing all pension *contributions* once, then treating benefits as tax-free income (see Chapter 3). In contrast, earnings used to purchase current health insurance are exempt from taxation at any time. This practice sets up a tax bias in favor of too much health insurance and too little consumption of other items.

For example, consider the numbers in the first two rows of Table 5–2. The numbers show that an individual facing a 15 percent income tax rate on income actually pays a 15 percent income tax on earnings used to purchase immediate non-health insurance consumption; but if earnings are used to purchase health insurance, a zero income tax is paid.[13] This difference in tax treatment creates a distortion that artificially reduces the apparent cost of health cost by 15 cents on each dollar spent.

Individuals at the 28 percent marginal tax rate face an even larger tax distortion: for each one dollar devoted to consumption items such as food, clothing, and education, only 72 cents remains after taxes are assessed. But if the same dollar is used to purchase health benefits, the entire one dollar is available for this consumption. This creates incentives to have "Cadillac" health benefits because the government makes it appear that they are available at "Ford" prices.

If workers faced the choice between spending an incremental 72 cents on more health benefits or on some other consumption item with-

TABLE 5–2 Tax Rates for Retiree Health Insurance

	Statutory Tax Rate	
Category	*15 Percent*	*28 Percent*
Immediate consumption		
Health insurance	0.0	0.0
Other	15.0	28.0
Age-65 consumption		
Health insurance		
Current tax policy	20.1	34.3
Pension parallel	15.0	28.0
Other		
Using pension	15.0	28.0
Not using pension	32.1	52.6

NOTE: Numbers in table are percents. Worker's current age is assumed to be 50; interest rate is 10 percent.

out effectively receiving a 28 cents rebate of sorts if they chose to purchase extra health insurance, workers might well prefer "Ford" policies at "Ford" prices. This means that they might have policies with more deductibles, fewer routine benefits, more outpatient care, etc. By subsidizing the real price of insurance coverage, all workers as a group pay for incremental coverage they do not fully value. In terms of Figure 2–1, which demonstrated the costs of government interference with market prices, the price of health insurance policies is artificially reduced, leading workers to purchase incremental units of coverage worth less than the cost of providing it.

The issue is not one affiliated with a redistribution of income or an encouragement of low-income workers to increase health coverage. Since low-income workers do not pay taxes, the thrust of these tax distortions is in the direction of encouraging primarily higher-income workers to have too much insurance coverage.

We can now consider use of wages to purchase health insurance policies during retirement. In effect, current tax policy does not extend the special tax-free treatment of investment earnings on pension savings to retiree health insurance. In effect, workers must save for this benefit outside a tax-exempt trust fund. Thus, while savings for retiree health benefits escape the so-called first tax on earnings, they are subject to the "second tax." For example, consider a 50-year-old worker saving for health insurance coverage at age 65. The interest rate and the inflation rate are 10 percent; the real rate of return is zero.

If the worker devotes one dollar of wages towards saving for these benefits that are offered by the corporation in fifteen years, he is not taxed on the original one dollar in wages. However, over time, this implicit savings, in effect, accumulates at a post-tax rate of return. The worker saves either at an 8.5 percent interest rate or 7.2 percent, depending upon whether he is in the 15 or 28 percent tax bracket. Since the inflation rate in the example is 10 percent, his savings will lose real value: at age 65, his original one dollar of real savings is worth either 79.9 or 65.7 cents depending on the tax rate. The effective tax rate on his original one dollar of savings for retiree health insurance is either 20.1 or 34.3 percent.

These effective tax rates would differ depending upon the interest rate and time period of savings. Current tax policy however, that attaches a "second tax" on earnings from implicit savings for retiree health insurance coverage is in the ballpark of an income tax attached to other wages at the time they are earned (these rates are 15 and 28 percent).

These numbers are shown in the bottom portion of Table 5–2. One dollar in earnings saved for retirement through a pension is taxed at the statutory income taxes rates equal to either 15 or 28 percent. As shown earlier (see Chapter 2), the same dollar saved outside the pension would face an effective tax rate equal to roughly twice these amounts, or 32.1 and 52.6 percent. In contrast, if the same dollar is saved for postretirement health benefits, it faces a tax rate equal to 20.1 or 34.3 percent.

If retiree health benefits are awarded tax-free accumulation, the price distortion towards immediate purchases of incremental insurance coverage is extended to the purchase of incremental insurance during retirement, thereby encouraging too much expenditure on retiree health coverage. *If tax-exempt status is awarded to retiree health benefits, then to put these benefits on a parallel treatment to pensions, the value of these policies should be included with pensions as taxable income during retirement; or implicit contributions to finance this insurance should be subject to taxation during work years.* The tax revenue implications of awarding tax-exempt status to retiree health savings accounts is roughly offset by additional revenues that would be generated by treating retiree health benefits as taxable income.

A better idea would be to eliminate all the distortions in the tax code that favor health insurance coverage.[14] This change could be effected by including the value of employer health insurance coverage as currently taxable income to workers. Similarly, the value of retiree health insurance coverage can be included as taxable income during retirement, and corporate contributions set aside to pay for retiree health coverage can be accumulated tax free. In this framework, workers' earnings, whether they are devoted to the purchase of immediate consumption or retirement consumption, and whether they are used to support extra insurance coverage or other consumption, all would be

TABLE 5–3 Parallel Treatment of Retiree Health Benefits

Category	*Current Policy*	*Parallel Policy to Pensions*
Health insurance policy for workers	Tax-exempt to corporations and individuals.	Include value as taxable income to individuals.
Health insurance policy for retirees	Same	Include value as taxable income to retirees.
Tax Status of health benefit trusts	Taxable	Tax-exempt

taxed at the same rates; and a true parallel would be created in the tax code between retiree health coverage and other pension savings. A summary of these proposals is listed in Table 5–3.

FINAL REMARKS

For historical reasons, tax policy towards pensions has been intertwined with a large body of companion regulation embodied in the social security system, pension law, and the tax code itself. The restrictions implicit in this regulatory framework has provided significant interference with free market retirement decisions. The federal government has recently made significant headway towards reducing these restrictions, giving workers and firms more influence over retirement decisions. These changes, most notably in the social security system, together with the central tenet of the tax code towards pensions (that is, consumption tax treatment of savings for retirement), has established "neutrality" as a principal theme for national retirement policy. This drift in policy undoubtedly has led to large economic benefits for current and future workers.

There are, however, additional changes in tax and regulatory policies that can enhance these benefits. These benefits can be generated by recognizing the neutrality principle as a main theme in national pension tax and retirement policy and applying it consistently. A central message of this volume is that movements in this direction can be done without interfering with a social security system that ensures at least a minimal level of retirement consumption for everyone, particularly low-income individuals.

Moreover, pursuit of this principle does not imply a conflict with the need to raise federal tax revenue. In fact, while most of the proposals in Table 5–1 would be expected to be revenue neutral, several would raise additional revenue (most notably the removal of income tax smoothing) while, at the same time, reducing economic distortions caused by current tax policy. Instead of pursuing a policy of raising miscellaneous revenues by interfering with various existing tax provisions for pensions on an ad hoc basis—and thereby threatening the viability of the current retirement system—the same revenue can be raised by building on the principle of neutrality, which has emerged as perhaps the most enlightened theme for a rational national retirement policy.

ENDNOTES

1. Penalties for retiring early were attributable to the so-called recalculation effect. Benefits were tied to average nominal wage histories back to 1951; thus, by working to later ages, workers significantly increased their annuities by replacing inflation-eroded earnings from the 1950s with more recent earnings. In 1977, the formula was changed so that benefits were tied to wage histories indexed to a national wage base.

   Retirement past age 65 was discouraged by an "earnings test." Social security benefits were offset by 50 cents for each one dollar of wages earned (beyond some threshold). Annuity amounts after age 65 were not actuarially fair: they did not offset the benefits lost by working one more year. In 1983, the system was changed so that by the year 2005, actuarially fair annuities will be paid for all ages after 62.
2. The problems of assigning contributions to workers in a defined benefit plan would be overwhelming, and would result in volatility in taxable income to individuals. In addition, a "rebate" system would have to be developed so that if workers quit, they could recapture taxes paid on the portion of their real accrued pension benefits lost upon quitting.
3. In addition, because the new limits make it impossible to prefund ad hoc post retirement inflation adjustments, the system biases firms to offer pension plans with contractual COLAs (which can be funded). The provision of contractual COLAs, together with initial benefits indexed to wages, makes it difficult for workers to share the downside of investment risk in the portfolio. As a result, benefits are expected to be lower for the same flow of implicit worker contributions, reflecting the loss of their share of the higher return derived from the risk premia embedded in riskier portfolios. In other words, the tax distortion in favor of less risky portfolios also works to reduce corresponding benefits in these plans.
4. These benefits should be defined to include anticipated levels of ad hoc post-retirement COLA policies based on experience in the plan.
5. Some of these assumptions might include quit rates, mortality rates, wage growth, and postretirement inflation adjustments.
6. ERISA itself does not impose important limitations on firms' choices of pension portfolios except, in most cases, to prevent investing more than 10 percent of assets in the plan sponsor's own securities and to diversify across many securities (which does not rule out all-stock or all-bond portfolios).
7. There are some exceptions. For example, workers covered by collective bargaining agreements can be covered by a separate plan.

8. Transitional relief is provided by permitting individuals to use the higher of $150,000 in nominal terms or $112,500 indexed to prices beginning in 1988.
9. Here *fraud* is defined to mean the firing of older workers just prior to vesting or termination of the pension plan midstream in the contract.
10. See Richard A. Ippolito, "Pension Security: Has ERISA Had Any Effect?" *Regulation* (No. 2 1987), pp. 15–22.
11. For example, there is no reason to afford tax policy to a high-wage earner who saves over his entire life or may have access to multiple pensions, and, at the same time, to constrain tax policy towards other high-wage earners who prefer to save disproportionately later in life, and who may have access to only one pension plan. In addition, the way the limits work in defined benefit plans, they may not be comparable with limits attached to defined contribution accounts, thereby creating the potential for bias in the choice of pension plan type.
12. I have dealt with the insurance issue extensively in Ippolito, *The Economics of Pension Insurance,* 1989.
13. Even though technically the insurance is purchased by the firm, it is part of the fringe benefits package that ultimately is provided at the expense of lower cash wages (see Chapter 1).
14. This idea has been espoused, for example, by Martin Feldstein, formerly Chairman of the Council of Economic Advisors.

Selected References

Trade-off between Wages and Pensions

Ehrenberg, Ronald G. "Retirement System Characteristics and Compensating Wage Differentials in the Public Sector." *Industrial Labor Relations Review* 33, 1980, pp. 470–483.

Ehrenberg, Ronald G.; and Robert Smith. *Modern Labor Economics*. Glenview, IL: Scott Foresman, 1985.

Schiller, Bradley R.; and Randall D. Weiss. "Pensions and Wages: A Test for Equalizing Differences." *Review of Economics and Statistics* 63, 1980, pp. 529–538.

Smith, Robert S. "Compensating Differentials for Pensions and Underfunding in the Public Sector." *Review of Economics and Statistics* 63, 1981, pp. 463–468.

Rate of Pension Savings over Tenure

Clark, Robert; and Ann A. McDermed. "Life Cycle Patterns of Earnings, Pension Wealth and Total Compensation." *Quarterly Journal of Economics* 101, 1986, pp. 341–362.

———. "Earnings Response to Pension Coverage and Eligibility." Paper presented at the American Economic Association Meetings, New York, 1985.

Ippolito, Richard A. "The Labor Contract and True Economic Pension Liabilities." *American Economic Review* 75, December 1985, pp. 1031–1043.

Mitchell, Olivia; and S. Pozzenbon. "Wages, Pensions, and the Wage-Pension Trade-off." Paper presented at the American Economic Association Meetings, New Orleans, 1986.

Pensions and Job Mobility

Allen, Steven; Robert Clark; and Daniel Sumner. "Job Mobility, Older Workers and the Role of Pensions." Final Report submitted to the U.S. Department of Labor, 1986.

Bartel, Ann P.; and George J. Borjas. "Middle-Age Job Mobility: Its Determinants and Consequences." In *Men in Their Pre-Retirement Years*. Philadelphia: Temple University School of Business Administration, 1977.

Ippolito, Richard A. "Why Federal Workers Don't Quit." *Journal of Human Resources* 22, Spring 1987, pp. 281–299.

Mitchell, Olivia S. "Fringe Benefits and Labor Mobility." *Journal of Human Resources* 17, Spring 1982, pp. 286–298.

Schiller, Bradley R.; and Randall D. Weiss. "The Impact of Private Pensions on Firm Attachments." *Review of Economics and Statistics* 62, 1980, pp. 369–380.

Pensions and Retirement Age

Burkhauser, Richard B. "The Pension Acceptance Decision of Older Workers." *Journal of Human Resources* 14, Winter 1979, pp. 63–75.

Fields, Gary; and Olivia Mitchell. *Retirement, Pensions, and Social Security.* Cambridge, Mass.: MIT Press, 1984.

Gustman, Alan L.; and Thomas L. Steinmeier. "A Structural Model of Retirement." *Econometrica* 54, May 1986, pp. 555–584.

Ippolito, Richard A. "Income Tax Policy and Lifetime Labor Supply." *Journal of Public Economics* 26, April 1985, pp. 327–347.

———, "Towards Explaining Earlier Retirement After 1970." *Industrial Labor Relations Review* 43, 1990, Forthcoming.

Pension Coverage and Benefits

Andrews, Emily. *The Changing Profile of Business in America.* Washington, D.C.: Employee Benefit Research Institute, 1985.

Beller, Daniel. "Coverage Patterns of Full-Time Employees under Private Retirement Plans." *Social Security Bulletin* 44, July 1981, pp. 3–11.

Clark, Robert; Steven Allen; and Daniel Sumner. "Postretirement Adjustments of Pensions." *Journal of Human Resources* 21, 1986, pp. 118–137.

Dorsey, Stuart. "A Model and Empirical Estimates of Worker Pension Coverage in the U.S." *Southern Economic Journal* 49, October 1982, pp. 506–520.

McCarthy, David. *Findings from the Survey of Private Pension Benefit Amounts.* U.S. Department of Labor. Washington, D.C., G.P.O, 1985.

Pensions and National Savings

Diamond, Peter A.; and Jerry A. Hausman. "Individual Retirement and Savings Behavior." *Journal of Public Economics* 23, February 1984, pp. 81–114.

Dicks-Mireaux, Louis; and Mervyn King. "Pension Wealth and Household Savings: Tests of Robustness." *Journal of Public Economics* 23, February 1984, pp. 115–140.

Feldstein, Martin. "Do Private Pensions Increase National Saving?" *Journal of Public Economics* 10, December 1978, pp. 277–293.

Munnell, Alicia. "Private Pensions and Saving: New Evidence." *Journal of Political Economy* 84, October 1976, pp. 1013–1031.

Pensions and Regulation

Clark, Robert; and Ann McDermed. *The Regulatory Impact on Defined Benefit Pension Plans*. Washington, D.C.: American Enterprise Institute, 1989, forthcoming.

Cornwell, Christopher; Stuart Dorsey; and Nasser Mehrzad. "Opportunistic Behavior by Firms in Implicit Pension Contracts." West Virginia University, Mimeograph, 1988.

Ippolito, Richard A. "A Study of the Regulatory Effect of the Employee Retirement Income Security Act." *Journal of Law and Economics* 31, April 1988, pp. 85–125.

———, *The Economics of Pension Insurance*. Homewood, IL: Richard D. Irwin (for the Pension Research Council), 1989.

Logue, Dennis. *Legislative Influence on Corporate Pension Plans*. Washington, D.C.: American Enterprise Institute, 1979.

Treynor, Jack; W. Priest; and P. Regan. *The Financial Reality of Pension Funding under ERISA*. Homewood, IL: Dow Jones-Irwin, 1976.

Pension Portfolios and Taxes

Black, Fisher. "The Tax Consequences of Long–Run Pension Policy." *Financial Analysts Journal* 36, July–August 1980, pp. 3–10.

Ippolito, Richard A. "The Role of Risk in a Tax Arbitrage Pension Portfolio." *Financial Analysts Journal* 46, Jan./Feb. 1990, Forthcoming.

Scholes, Myron; and Mark Wolfson. *Taxes and Business Strategy: A Global Planning Approach*. Prentice-Hall, 1989.

Sharpe, William. "Corporate Pension Policy." *Journal of Financial Economics* 3, June 1976, pp. 183–193.

Tepper, Irwin. "Taxation and Corporate Pension Policy." *Journal of Finance* 36, March 1981, pp. 1–14.

Treynor, Jack L. "The Principles of Corporate Pension Finance." *Journal of Finance* 32, May 1977, pp. 627–638.

Social Security System

Blinder, Alan; Roger Gordon; and Donald Wise. "Reconsidering the Work Disincentives of Social Security." *National Tax Journal* 33, December 1980, pp. 431–442.

Boskin, Michael; and Douglas Puffert. "The Financial Impact of Social Security by Cohort under Alternative Financing Assumptions." National Bureau of Economic Research, Working Paper No. 2225, April 1987.

Burtless, Gary. "Social Security, Unanticipated Benefit Increases and the Timing of Retirement." *Review of Economic Studies* 53, October 1986, pp. 781–805.

Burkhauser, Richard V. "The Early Acceptance of Social Security: An Asset Maximization Approach." *Industrial Labor Relations Review* 33, 1980, pp. 484–492.

——— and John Turner. "Can 25 Million Americans Be Wrong? A Response to Blinder, Gordon, and Wise." *National Tax Journal* 34, December 1981, pp. 467–472.

Feldstein, Martin. "Social Security, Induced Retirement, and Aggregate Capital Accumulation." *Journal of Political Economy* 82, September 1974, pp. 905–926.

Moffitt, Robert. "Trends in Social Security Wealth by Cohort." In *Economic Transfers in the United States*, edited by M. Moon. Chicago: University of Chicago Press, 1977.

Munnell, Alicia. *The Future of Social Security*. Washington, D.C.: Brookings Institution, 1977.

Social Security Administration. *Social Security Bulletin—Annual Statistical Supplement*, 1987.

Consumption Tax

Aaron, Henry J.; Harvey Galper; and Joseph A. Pechman, eds. *Uneasy Compromise: Problems of a Hybrid Income–Consumption Tax*. Washington, D.C.: Brookings Institution, 1988.

Auerbach, Alan; and Martin Feldstein. *Handbook of Public Finance*. Amsterdam: North Holland, 1985.

Bradford, David F. *Blueprints for Basic Tax Reform*. Washington, D.C.: U.S. Department of the Treasury, 1977.

Fullerton, Don; John B. Shoven; and John Walley. "Replacing the U.S. Income Tax with a Progressive Consumption Tax." *Journal of Public Economics* 20, 1983, pp. 3–23.

Kaldor, Nicholas. *An Expenditure Tax*. London: Allen and Unwin, 1955.

Hall, Robert; and Alvin Rabushka. *The Flat Tax*. Stanford: Hoover Institution Press, 1985.

Makin, John. *Real Tax Reform: Replacing the Income Tax*. Washington, D.C.: American Enterprise Institute, 1985.

Pechman, Joseph A. *Federal Tax Policy*. 5th ed., Washington, D.C.: Brookings Institution, 1987.

Walker, Charles; and Mark Bloomfield. *The Consumption Tax: A Better Alternative*. Cambridge: Ballinger, 1987.

Other References

Allen, E.; J. Melone; J. Rosenbloom; and J. VanDerhei. *Pension Planning*. Homewood, IL: Richard D. Irwin, 1988.

Beller, Daniel; and John Turner. eds. *Trends in Pensions*. U.S. Department of Labor (G.P.O.), 1989.

Congressional Budget Office, *Tax Policy for Pensions and Other Retirement Savings*. April 1987.

Davis, Kingsley. "Retirement as a Dubious Paradise—Another Point of View." In *Issues in Contemporary Retirement* edited by E. Lazear and R. Ricardo Campbell. Stanford, CA: Hoover Institution, 1988.

Ippolito, Richard A. *Pensions, Economics, and Public Policy*. Homewood, IL: Dow Jones-Irwin (for the Pension Research Council), 1986.

——— and Walter Kolodrubetz. *The Handbook of Pension Statistics*. Chicago: Commerce Clearing House, 1986.

Latimar, Murray. *Industrial Pension Systems*. New York: Industrial Relations Counselors, 1932.

McGill, Dan M.; and Donald S. Grubbs. *Fundamentals of Private Pensions*, 6th ed., Homewood, IL: Richard D. Irwin, 1989.

Wyatt & Co., *Survey of Actuarial Assumptions and Funding*. Washington, D.C.: Wyatt & Co., 1988.

Appendix Tables

TABLE A–1 Pension Assets, 1950–1987

Year	*Total*	*Private*	*State and Local Gov't*
1950	$ 70	$ 49	$ 21
1955	147	105	42
1960	255	186	69
1965	427	315	112
1970	547	386	161
1975	738	536	202
1980	1,033	783	250
1985	1,523	1,133	390
1987	1,836*	1,358	478

*$2,008 in billions of 1987 dollars.

NOTE: Numbers in the table are in billions of constant 1984 dollars.

SOURCES: R. Ippolito and W. Kolodrubetz, eds. *The Handbook of Pension Statistics*; and D. Beller and J. Turner, eds., *Trends in Pensions.*

TABLE A–2 Pension Share of Financial Assets

Year	Total Financial Assets	Corporate Equity
1950	3.0	0.9
1955	4.4	2.2
1960	6.3	4.1
1965	7.5	6.3
1970	8.9	9.6
1975	12.2	17.8
1980	15.0	19.3
1985	16.8	21.6
1987	17.8	23.8

NOTE: Numbers in table are percents.

SOURCE: see Table A–1.

TABLE A–3 Defined Contribution Plan Assets

Year	*Percent**
1950	11.6
1955	14.7
1960	18.0
1965	20.8
1970	23.4
1975	25.7
1980	27.8
1987	37.5

*Share of total private pension plan assets.

SOURCE: Richard A. Ippolito, *Pensions, Economics and Public Policy,* p. 114, and unpublished data (for 1987 only) from the U.S. Department of Labor.

TABLE A–4 Distribution of Termination Funding Ratios, 1978–1986

	Percent Participants								
Funding Ratio	*1978*	*1979*	*1980*	*1981*	*1982*	*1983*	*1984*	*1985*	*1986*
0–24%	.8	.8	2.4	.3	.3	.3	.3	.3	2.0
25–49	8.8	9.7	3.8	2.6	2.5	2.0	1.6	1.8	1.4
50–74	14.2	16.0	11.5	8.3	8.0	7.6	2.8	3.7	4.5
75–99	24.6	26.5	17.1	10.4	9.3	6.7	9.0	9.5	7.0
100–124	25.5	25.8	22.9	14.1	14.2	13.4	10.1	11.7	13.3
125–149	14.9	11.7	22.1	20.1	19.5	18.2	12.2	16.5	19.2
150 +	11.1	9.2	22.0	44.1	46.1	51.7	63.8	56.4	52.6
Average	92.9%	88.5	107.2	128.8	130.9	139.2	153.9	145.6	140.2
Underfunding ($1986)*	$116.7	126.0	73.0	42.1	39.5	35.8	25.9	31.8	30.8
Interest Rate†	7.25	7.50	8.75	10.25	10.75	9.25	10.0	9.75	7.75

SOURCE: Form 5500 Annual Pension Plan Reports.

*Underfunding is adjusted to 1986 dollars and size of pension universe. Funding ratios are calculated for each year using a constant 2 percent discount rate. Assets in year t are then set equal to assets in 1986, times the real funding ratio in year t, divided by the same ratio in 1986. Liabilities in year t are set equal to those in 1986 but adjusted to the PBGC immediate annuity rates shown in the table.

†Average PBGC immediate annuity rate during year.

TABLE A–5 Distribution of Ongoing Funding Ratios, 1978–1986

	Percent Participants								
Funding Ratio	*1978*	*1979*	*1980*	*1981*	*1982*	*1983*	*1984*	*1985*	*1986*
0–24%	2.8	3.3	2.4	2.0	2.0	.9	.8	.9	2.5
25–49	16.5	22.2	15.3	13.1	13.2	10.4	10.0	10.1	4.6
50–74	36.4	39.5	34.9	27.5	27.6	18.6	16.9	17.1	13.3
75–99	30.2	25.6	31.1	32.1	33.2	29.3	27.3	28.1	26.8
100–124	9.1	6.1	10.6	16.4	16.4	24.4	25.6	25.1	24.3
125–149	2.6	2.0	3.0	5.2	5.1	9.8	11.2	11.0	15.4
150 +	2.4	1.3	2.7	3.8	3.6	6.5	8.0	7.6	13.1
Average	65.3	60.3	67.3	74.4	74.1	84.3	87.5	86.5	94.9
Underfunding ($1986)*	$343.0	387.5	325.8	268.5	272.4	203.5	187.6	191.3	184.9

SOURCE: Form 5500 Annual Pension Plan Reports.

*Underfunding is adjusted to 1986 dollars and size of pension universe, as described in notes to Table A–4, except liabilities in all years are fixed at 1986 levels.

Index